INHABITATION IN NATURE

Houses, People and Practices

David Clapham

First published in Great Britain in 2023 by

Policy Press, an imprint of
Bristol University Press
University of Bristol
1–9 Old Park Hill
Bristol
BS2 8BB
UK
t: +44 (0)117 374 6645
e: bup-info@bristol.ac.uk

Details of international sales and distribution partners are available at policy.bristoluniversitypress.co.uk

© Bristol University Press 2023

British Library Cataloguing in Publication Data
A catalogue record for this book is available from the British Library

ISBN 978-1-4473-6780-2 hardcover
ISBN 978-1-4473-6782-6 ePub
ISBN 978-1-4473-6783-3 ePdf

The right of David Clapham to be identified as author of this work has been asserted by him in accordance with the Copyright, Designs and Patents Act 1988.

Cover design: Liam Roberts
Image credit: iStock/Jakub Rutkiewicz
Bristol University Press and Policy Press use environmentally responsible print partners.
Printed and bound in Great Britain by CPI Group (UK) Ltd, Croydon, CR0 4YY

FSC
www.fsc.org
MIX
Paper | Supporting
responsible forestry
FSC® C013604

This book is dedicated to Ravi, Lizzie, Hannah, Kieran and Belinda, and especially to my grandchildren Tipene, Sammy, AJ and Layla who are a source of endless joy.

Contents

Preface

I was reminded recently that I have been teaching, researching and writing about housing for more than 45 years. During that astonishingly long period of time my ideas and approaches have changed considerably as I have been on a personal journey of discovery on which this book is a further (and hopefully not final) step. In discussions on the book with colleagues, it was suggested that I try to outline the main elements in this enjoyable and absorbing journey and, in particular, to describe how this latest step relates to those that preceded it in order to further understanding of the ideas in the book and my reasons for thinking that they are important.

I graduated with a degree in business studies which gave me a good grounding in many of the social sciences including economics, sociology, psychology and politics. After some time working on housing issues in local government, I returned to study social administration and did my PhD on policy planning in local government. With this background it is not surprising that my early research in housing had a very interdisciplinary and empirical focus and reflected my continuing concern with the implications of research for policy and practice. However, I was soon influenced by my friend Jim Kemeny to apply social theory in my work. Unsure where to look for this, I turned to social constructionism, which was his adopted framework and one that I had studied in my undergraduate days where I developed an interest in phenomenology as a research philosophy. Berger and Luckmann's *The Social Construction of Reality* was my source of knowledge and inspiration in this work and I tried to apply the ideas in my research on housing management and other areas. Along with a growing understanding of the constraints and contradictions of that approach, I became increasingly interested in some 'postmodern' sociologists such as Bourdieu, Beck and, in particular, Giddens. I was heavily influenced by the concept of structuration that promised to make a major contribution to resolving the long-standing agency/structure division that dominated sociology. Giddens' writing introduced me to the concept of social practices that has underpinned my work since and to which I have returned in the present book. I attempted to bring together the elements of social constructionism, with its emphasis on meaning, with structuration and its focus on agency and structure through the study of social practices in *The Meaning of Housing* with its foundational concept of the housing pathway based on these different elements.

At the time I was very happy with the fusion of the ideas and it has given me a base on which to ground further work that has proved to be a development rather than a refutation of these ideas. However, I became increasingly haunted by the limitations of the frameworks I had used. When in my favourite place, sitting on a mountain-top with no one else in sight, I became puzzled by the emphasis in social constructionism on social interaction and language in creating meaning and reality. How did I know I existed in this time and place and sitting alone on this very material structure surrounded by other forms of life whether flora or fauna? Therefore, a continuing problem was the overemphasis on language in social constructionism, which dominated my thoughts and led to me becoming engaged in many debates about the nature of the so-called 'material world' and how it should be incorporated into housing analysis, which at its core is about the relationship between people and their physical environment of the dwelling. My first attempt to solve these issues came through the introduction by another friend, Henny Coolen, to the ideas on the psychology of perception by Gibson (1979) and his concept of the 'affordances' that people perceive in their environment. I applied this approach in my research and writing on housing and support for vulnerable people in the book *Accommodating Difference*, and interest in this concept has extended to this volume.

During my academic journey the situation in housing and other public policies has changed significantly. Dissatisfaction with the direction of policy from the 1990s onward with its basis in neoliberal thought and its severe impact on the lives of many people led to the publication of *Remaking Housing Policy*, which, among other things, wrestled with the problems of defining evaluation criteria to decide a 'good' policy. Although I had explored ideas of subjective wellbeing and the capabilities approach before, it became apparent that there were difficulties in applying these approaches to issues of environmental sustainability. The question I was left with was how to define a good housing policy that met environmental objectives.

At each stage in the journey I have tried to keep the virtues of the previous steps, but to extend them and to integrate them with other perspectives. As a consequence, *Inhabitation in Nature* contains each of the elements I have outlined here. The book was stimulated by the climate change crisis and the global COVID-19 epidemic, but also by a personal love of mountains and wilderness, and an active concern for environmental issues that goes back to the 1970s. This chimed with my wish to build on the discussion of social practices and the pathways approach in *The Meaning of Housing* by incorporating a material element. In reacquainting myself with the literature on social practices I realised that it had moved on extensively from the work of Giddens and had incorporated many of the concerns about materiality that had troubled me. Therefore, a framework existed for the book that could be adopted while developing rather than superseding the previous work.

As with previous stages in my intellectual journey, having completed the book, I am left with a feeling of much distance still to be travelled. I have been concerned by the shortage of material in many areas and topics and this has shaped the book and resulted in a very general coverage of the issues without the specific studies that would have resulted in more detailed and practical discussion and policy recommendations. The hope is that the book will stimulate the much-needed research. Also, I am particularly troubled by my lack of understanding of issues outside the social sciences. Having called in the book for a holistic approach to the study of people in Nature, I am very aware of my shortcomings in being able to undertake such an enterprise because of my lack of knowledge about the material world. I currently live on a croft on the Isle of Skye and have a personal project to rewild and reforest some of this land. I am looking to this and the research and reading associated with it to widen my horizons and to give me some concepts from other sciences to add to the framework outlined here. Perhaps my next book will be on trees!

None of the individual ideas in this book are original, but the major contribution lies in their integration and their application to the context of housing studies. The result is a radical call for the refocusing of the field of study and a review of the scope of research and the frameworks and methods used. The book is intended to raise awareness of the need for research on inhabitation that will contribute to knowledge on how people can be a considerate and empathetic part of Nature and cope with the major issues that confront the world today, such as climate change and the lack of biodiversity. Hopefully readers will find it a stimulating contribution to their own thinking and research.

As with all journeys, the intellectual one described here has involved interaction with a large number of people who have influenced my thinking and some of whom I have already mentioned. For the latest work explored in this book I am particularly indebted to two colleagues at Swinburne University in Melbourne, Melissa Pineda Pinto and Barbara Bok, who stimulated the early thinking on the topic and encouraged me to investigate theories and fields that were new to me. Thank you both!

David Clapham
Glasgow
July 2022

Introduction: Inhabitation in Nature

The relationship between people and what for ease of exposition at this point I will call the rest of Nature is a common talking point in the media and political debate. Recently, climate change and the COVID-19 pandemic have brought the issues involved into sharp relief and houses, and the way we live in them, are often included in debates about mitigating climate change or coping with the pandemic. We are exhorted to 'stay at home' to avoid spreading infection and to use less energy to heat our homes to avert climate change. However, the theme of this book is that these issues are relatively neglected in research and policy in the housing field, partly because of the lack of a coherent and widely accepted framework for analysing the issues involved. Therefore, the aim of this book is to formulate a framework for thinking about housing processes and outcomes, as well as the policies and programmes of housing agencies and governments, which considers the relationship between people, their homes and the physical, biological and material context or Nature. Emphasis on the links between living in houses and Nature is not new. Architects such as Frank Lloyd Wright and Alvar Aalto have drawn attention to some of the issues involved that have influenced their designs. The philosopher John Dewey has discussed the importance of inhabitation in a place in the process of learning and developed his view of the aims of education from this base. However, the argument here is that there is a lack of a coherent framework to investigate the issues involved in a way that can be studied and form the basis of policy. Some frameworks already exist that claim to do this, but as will become apparent throughout the discussion here, they each have their problems and shortcomings that need to be overcome. Further, it is argued that such an approach is necessary to understand issues that have been the traditional focus of housing research and policy, such as homelessness or affordability, that have rarely been considered to be related to climate change or other 'environmental' challenges. In other words, the ambitious aim in this book is to provide a universal framework for housing research and policy. It is hoped that, at the very least, the book will provide a useful stimulus for debate on the important issues involved.

The central argument of the book consists of four propositions:

1. Houses and the people that live in them are important elements of Nature rather than separated from it.

2. The concept of 'inhabitation' provides an appropriate focus for what has been previously called housing studies and policy.
3. The practices of everyday living in houses (inhabitation practices) are the key focus of research and are the primary foundation for the making of housing policy.
4. Analysis of inhabitation practices needs to adopt a holistic approach to knowledge and the requisite research methods and techniques employed.

The first two propositions are the focus of this introductory chapter that sets the groundwork for the analysis that follows. The next two chapters focus on the third proposition by examining the strengths and weaknesses of existing and potential approaches for studying the processes of inhabitation such as social constructionism and new materialism, before considering in depth the concept of practices that forms the approach adopted here. These two chapters discuss the theoretical frameworks used to analyse housing, focusing on those that include animal and material elements. The 'practices' approach advocated here is one that is seeing increased prominence in debates in the social sciences in general (see Chapter 3) and, when combined with the concept of inhabitation, provides the concept of inhabitation practices that forms the cornerstone of the book. Chapter 4 focuses on the fourth proposition by discussing the issues involved in the analysis of inhabitation practices and highlighting the issues and choices involved.

The next three chapters are intended to illustrate how the framework identified here can be used by focusing on specific examples of the inhabitation practices involved in the consumption and production of houses as well as those outside the home itself. In these final chapters of the book, examples will be provided of the relationship between housing policy and practice and the rest of Nature based on current knowledge and to identify the topics for further research using the inhabitation practices framework advocated here. It is important to make clear at this stage that current knowledge is partial and in need of continued monitoring and updating. The contents of the book are based on secondary sources as the requisite new empirical research would take a number of research programmes and many years to undertake. Therefore, a primary theme of the book is the importance of developing a framework for research that needs to be undertaken on an ongoing basis at different geographical levels and in different social, economic and political as well as geographical contexts in order to inform policymaking.

A revised framework is important if key policy challenges such as climate change and decreasing biodiversity are to be met and the role of housing in these issues is to be understood. A change of approach is needed because, as Horne (2018: 42) comments: 'Housing scholars have been slow to link the core topics of affordable housing and universal housing provision to concerns about climate change.' The contention of this book is that the slowness has, at least in part, been due to the approaches adopted by housing scholars. The inhabitation practices framework advocated here will help to explicate the links between housing and issues such as climate change, but it will also add important and neglected elements to traditional housing issues such as the affordability of housing, the assessment of housing quality or homelessness.

It is argued in the book that housing issues need to be seen in a different way and there is a need for alternative forms of policy to meet the challenges ahead and this should be based on sound knowledge of the complexities involved if it is to be successful. It will also need an engagement with the interests that shape current policy in housing issues and an understanding of the impact that they have and how they can be challenged.

People, houses and Nature

As Taylor et al (2020) point out, it is common to consider Nature to be in opposition to modern human life in cities. In this view, cities, where most people live, are seen as artificially built concrete environments that are the least green places and the antithesis of Nature that is seen in green fields. Moore (2015) argues that this modern thinking is based on a Cartesian narrative that places Nature and society in different domains. Therefore, modern society 'emerged *out* of Nature. It drew wealth *from* Nature. It disrupted, degraded, or defiled *Nature*. And now, or very soon, Nature will exact its revenge' (Moore, 2015: 5, original emphasis). Ingold argues that the Cartesian fractures between man and nature

> ultimately seem to derive from a single, underlying fault upon which the entire edifice of Western thought and science has been built – namely that which separates the 'two worlds' of humanity and nature. For this is what has given us the overriding academic division of labour between the disciplines that deal, on the one hand, with the human mind and its manifold linguistic, social and cultural products, and on the other, with the structures and composition of the material world. (Ingold, 2000: 1)

In a similar vein, Von Maltzahn (1994) argues that we tend to see Nature through the lens of the concepts of naturalism, positivism and objectivism in which Nature is represented in its outer form from the standpoint of the central human viewer who is seen as a neutral and passive observer rather than as an active participant.

Moore (2015), in an analysis with which we concur, sees the view of people as separate from Nature as toxic and responsible for a view of the material and animal environment as solely being a means for the meeting of human needs that has resulted in many current problems such as climate change. The separation of people and their houses and other built forms from Nature reinforces the view that climate change (and other problems such as disease epidemics and animal extinctions) are somehow divorced from human action. In this view, the study of climate change is the focus of the natural sciences and will be solved through scientific interventions that are somehow independent of human practices and lifestyles. The importance of social science is thus neglected, resulting in problems such as the reliance on technical solutions for energy efficiency that fail in reducing energy use because of human practices, such as turning the heating up when it becomes more efficient or cheaper or leaving windows open (see Chapter 5 for a fuller discussion).

The alternative view of the interrelatedness of people and Nature has a long history. For example, Patra (2006) discusses the *Vaastu Shastra* tradition of architecture in India, prevalent from 1500 to 1000 BC, which laid out fundamental principles that determined the orientation of a building, site layout, proportions of the building, use and position of rooms and so on. The approach is based on taking advantage of the five basic elements (earth, water, fire, air and space) in a way that brings balance and harmony between people, Nature and a building, thereby ensuring peace, prosperity and happiness. Patra (2006) compares this system with more recent writings of Heidegger (1971) on the concept of dwelling and building and notes the similarities. Heidegger argues that the aim of building is to use the five elements to enable 'dwelling', which is seen as a way of 'being in the world' and of living 'comfortably and beautifully':

> Buildings are not ends in themselves, but mediating objects through which we create a world for ourselves and enter into a dialogue with the world around us by defining and articulating our relationship to our fellow beings, nature and its phenomena, and 'the world beyond'. As such they involve the totality of our existence and our being, not a reductive, objectified notion of it. The earth that grounds us and all things, and provides the material for our building; the sky, the origin of space; the sun that animates all life and gives us the measure of time; the diurnal rhythm of night and day, light and dark; the dynamic cycle of the seasons and the climate; these are the primary components of architecture, not their derivatives of function, space, structure and form. (Heidegger, 1971: 147)

Heidegger's analysis has been influential in the philosophy and practice of some architecture and the concern with the place of dwellings in Nature can be seen in current design guides that include this element along with social, economic and aesthetic considerations (see, for example, Quality of

Life Foundation, nd) as well as in the work of acclaimed architects such as Frank Lloyd Wright and Alvar Aalto.

Taylor et al (2020) view all human activity as part of a web of life or an assemblage of ecologies, and cities are just one of these. All are part of Nature and need an integrated science to understand them. Investigating cities and houses is investigating Nature. Maller (2018: 1) argues that 'cities may appear to be all about humans, but entangled relationships and encounters between people and innumerable "non-humans" are at the heart of most urban challenges'. She uses the term non-humans to include 'any species, materials, matters, technologies or entities that can be artificially distinguished, partially or wholly, momentarily or more permanently, from humans' (Maller, 2018: 1). Examples are 'various non-human animals, plants, fungi, microbes, atoms, molecules, energies and waters' (Maller, 2018: 1).

Imrie argues:

> People are part of nature and in intervening in, and changing, the nature of natural materials, people are acting upon themselves, and the habitats and species that they depend on for their survival and well-being. Such actions do not destroy nature per se, but they can change its form and dynamics in ways that can challenge, even threaten, the survival of species, including the human race. (Imrie, 2021: 317–318)

In this spirit, Wilber (2000) uses the term Nature to include humans, animals and materials and this terminology is followed in the book, although animal and material elements will often be referred to in order to differentiate them from the human element and to expand analysis to include more than the usually dominant human aspect of any issue (for a fuller explanation of this use see Chapter 4, which also discusses the often-used term of an ecosystem). Here the terms human, animal and material are used to highlight the breadth of Nature and natural phenomena, but are not meant as tight or exclusive categories. Clearly humans are also animals and are made up of material elements, as are animals. The division between animals and materials is difficult to draw. Are viruses or bacteria animals or materials? Where should the division be drawn between the two categories? Plants are included in the material category, but are clearly different from granite, for example, because they have some aspects of 'life'. The distinctions the categorisation requires raise important and interesting issues, and will be discussed further in Chapter 4, but are beyond the scope of our discussion at this point. It will suffice here to note that the constituent elements of Nature are wide-ranging and diverse, and the term Nature with a capital letter is used to emphasise its all-encompassing scope which goes beyond the common usage of the term nature.

Ingold places emphasis on the links between the three elements of Nature:

> If human beings on the one hand, and plants and animals on the other, can be regarded alternately as components of each-others' environments, then we can no longer think of humans as inhabiting a social world of their own, over and above the world of nature in which the lives of all other living things are contained. Rather, both humans and the animals and plants on which they depend for a livelihood must be regarded as fellow participants in the same world, a world that is at once social and natural. And the forms that all these creatures take are neither given in advance nor imposed from above, but emerge within the context of their mutual involvement in a single, continuous field of relationships. (Ingold, 2000: 87)

The relationship between the three identified elements (human, animal and material) is an important one facing areas of public life and the government policies that are part of their construction, but a focus on housing is justified because of its impact on lifestyles, energy use and biodiversity issues. Housing (in the broadest sense) is an influential factor in how people live their lives and the impact that this has on the rest of Nature. The extent and importance of the factors that need to be considered in the relationship of housing as part of Nature will be explored more systematically later in the book, but one element that has received some recent consideration is the impact of houses on climate change. The Australian bushfires in early January 2020 provide an example of an event that demonstrates that the natural and physical world, houses, people and politics are inseparably linked in a highly controversial and fluid situation. During the early weeks of January 2020 in Australia, social media sites and newspapers covered stories of human and animal actors embroiled in vigorous actions and reactions, saving bushland everywhere from threatening human houses and farm animals. Koalas were pictured standing next to firefighters watching burning bushes and drinking from water wells alongside pets. Scientists were reported as expressing grave concerns over insect losses, and politicians and firefighters were at loggerheads over backburning to help prevent the spread of the fires. People who lost their houses were reported as angrily demonstrating against various levels of politicians and government over their inaction over climate change. It was later reported (*The Guardian*, 2020a) that over three billion animals had been killed or displaced during the outbreaks of 2019/2020 with a key contributing factor for the fires being considered to be the 'manic land grab' for new settlements and other development. It was labelled as the most dramatic loss of habitat for threatened species and devastation of ecological communities in postcolonial history. It was reported that 49 native species not currently listed as threatened could now be at risk, while government data suggested 471 plant and 191 invertebrate species needed urgent attention.

The COVID-19 outbreak provides another example of the limitations of our understanding that the links between houses, homes and the rest of the natural and physical world are far-reaching and very important to humans and other creatures. A key insight from the current epidemic and similar ones in the recent past (such as SARS and MERS) is that there is an increasing risk of the transfer of viruses from animals to humans. The highest chance of this happening is in areas of human activity such as newly cleared forest and new settlements where the habitat of wild animals is threatened, resulting in them being more prone to harmful viruses and leading to an increase in the opportunities for contact with humans. *The Guardian* (2020b) reported on a study that found that the human destruction of natural ecosystems increases the numbers of rats, bats and other animals that harbour diseases that can lead to pandemics such as COVID-19. The research assessed nearly 7,000 animal communities on six continents and found that the conversion of wild places into farmland or settlements often wipes out larger species. It found that the damage benefits smaller, more adaptable creatures that also carry the most pathogens that can pass to humans.

These examples show the different ways in which human interaction with the rest of Nature can have important impacts. The current political focus tends to be on climate change, but as Haraway argues:

[I]t's more than climate change, it's also extraordinary burdens of toxic chemistry, mining, depletion of lakes and rivers under and above ground, ecosystem simplification, vast genocides of people and other critters that threaten multiple, major system collapses. These losses will affect the health and well-being of numerous generations of humans and non-human species alike, and we are unlikely to understand the impacts on our health and the world's ecosystems until it is too late. The reason for this is our understanding of cities that prevents us from seeing humans as part of ecosystems. (Haraway, 2015: 159, quoted in Maller, 2018: 153)

Living in any dwelling in any place involves interaction with the outside human, material and animal world. These may be a threat to valued activities of everyday life (as in the bushfire or COVID-19 examples) or may be valued opportunities to walk in forests or green places or to grow vegetables or flowers. Any dwelling is the place of living for some humans and some animals, whether these are pets (Power, 2012, 2017) or other (perhaps unwelcome) animals such as spiders or mice. Of course, any material space is the home of millions of simple living organisms such as viruses and bacteria (as is the human body), some of which will be useful to humans and some less so. In the latter category one can think of moulds that may lead to an unhealthy living environment for humans. As Maller argues:

Although not always visible or noticed, vibrant non-humans are very much part of cities and similarly urbanised settings – in the water that flows through drains and pipes; in rock and other ancient substrates under asphalt and concrete – furthermore, insects, animals, birds, trees and other types of vegetation persist and innumerable microbes are found everywhere. Yet simplified binaries between humans and other species, and cities and 'wild' (or rural) landscapes, for example, persist and continue to be replicated in most urban policy, planning and research. (Maller, 2018: 153)

Ingold compares the similarities between a tree and a house. Although the tree may seem to provide shelter for many animals:

[T]he house also has many and diverse animal inhabitants – more, perhaps, than we are inclined to recognise. Sometimes special provision is made for them, such as the kennel, stable or dovecote. Others find shelter and sustenance in its nooks and crannies, or even build there. And all, in their various ways, contribute to its evolving form, as do the house's human inhabitants in keeping it under repair, decorating it, or making structural alterations in response to their changing domestic circumstances. Thus the distinction between the house and the tree is not an absolute but a relative one – relative, that is, to the scope of human involvement in the form-generating process. Houses, as Suzanne Blier notes (1987: 2), are living organisms. Like trees, they have life-histories, which consist in the unfolding of their relations with both human and non-human components of their environments. To the extent that the influence of the human component prevails, any feature of the environment will seem more like a building; to the extent that the nonhuman component prevails, it will seem less so. (Ingold, 2000: 187)

Whether harmful or a source of pleasure, the interactions between humans and non-humans have a massive impact on humans and animals and should be included in any analysis of living arrangements. Therefore, definitions of the scope of the field of housing studies and policy that focus purely on the house or home, or focus entirely on economic considerations, need to be revised to include the perspective that houses and homes are part of Nature and need to be defined and evaluated on that basis.

It does not need bushfires or other catastrophic events to demonstrate the intricate webs of relations of human housing with the rest of Nature and politics. At any time in the media one can read about how gardens enrich the house habitats in advertisements by nursery organisations, how developers of properties are wining and dining politicians to gain access to new land allocations (meaning bushland or countryside is transferred to housing land), and how people on very low incomes have to wait for years on housing lists, and more. The links are well summed up by Tony Juniper, who was the Chair of Natural England, a government body established to advise the British government on environmental issues, when he responded to government pronouncements on removing controls on new housing development to increase the number of new houses built. He referred to his argument that the health of the environment was crucial to the economy, to reduce flood risk, to improve public health wellbeing and to attract tourism. Therefore, the protection of nature should be at the heart of the development planning process (Juniper, 2013).

The attempt to remedy the narrow focus of much research and policy on housing starts in this chapter with a discussion of the ways of framing housing questions and setting the aims of housing policy, followed by the elements that should be considered in evaluating the success of policy and in judging housing outcomes. The discussion focuses on the importance of material and animal elements to the success of housing outcomes and policy.

How should housing be identified, defined and judged?

What is housing and how should we define the field of housing and housing policy? What is good housing? How can we tell whether housing arrangements are improving or getting better? How can we evaluate the impacts that housing arrangements have on residents, the wider population or the rest of Nature? The questions are key for those analysing housing issues and thus for the academic field of housing studies. Also, these are key questions for people who wish to better their own lives and for those who have a consideration for the impact of their practices on others and have values that they wish to live by. The questions are also vital for organisations involved in the production and consumption of housing, which need ways of defining their scope of action and measuring the impact of their activities. The argument here is that the usual ways of answering these questions are not well tuned to the current situation facing residents, housing organisations and governments because they do not address the role of housing as part of Nature. It is argued that a change of focus is needed if we are to answer these questions adequately. However, a coherent language and framework to examine this is lacking. As Maller (2018: 4) notes, '[c]oncepts and theories are required that decentre humans and embrace complexity, emergence and process, as well as those that overtly seek to cross or transcend disciplinary boundaries'. The task in this section is to outline some of the common ways that housing is defined and judged and to lay the ground for the discussion in the rest of the book of an alternative focus.

Before engaging with the issues, it is necessary to define the term housing policy, which can sometimes be used to solely refer to national governments. However, here, policy is viewed as being made through networks consisting of a number of public, private, voluntary and hybrid agencies (for a more detailed exposition of the position see Clapham, 2019). It is important for governments and public and private agencies involved in housing policy networks to understand and to articulate what they are trying to achieve. What are the scope and aims of housing policy or any housing programme? How does any housing agency know they are achieving success? How do the actions of one agency impact on the outcomes of the network as a whole? For simplicity henceforth, the focus here will be on a national housing policy, but bear in mind that the same arguments apply for the different agencies identified and at different geographical levels. Also, it is important to recognise that the impact of housing policies depends on the everyday practices of individuals and organisations that form the focus of the book. In this sense, the everyday practices of residents are an important element of policymaking and need to be included in any discussion of policies and their impact (see Chapter 4 for a fuller discussion of this point).

A dominant view in housing policy and housing studies is to view houses as an economic good that is bought and sold in a market. This view may coincide with that of some private organisations where there may be a simple economic and market-oriented answer to questions about their scope and impact, such as the extent of profit or market share. However, for public agencies with an obligation to pursue the public good, the answer may be more complex. National governments, state agencies or local governments charged with responsibility for the housing of the population in their area need some yardstick for judging whether they have succeeded and whether the contribution of other agencies in a policy network, such as private companies, contributes to this aim over and above issues of individual profitability. An individual agency, especially one with a profit motive or financial constraints, is likely to have an economic and financial motivation that leads it to focus on the financial costs and benefits to it of any action. Governments have also sometimes focused solely on economic and financial elements in their definition of the scope and evaluation of housing and other public policies. In this perspective, housing is seen as predominantly an economic good that is bought and sold in markets and can be defined and judged on economic and market criteria. Where financial imperatives are all-important the usual response is to focus on the monetary costs and benefits and this has been reinforced in the tendency in cost–benefit analysis in general to monetise benefits as it is argued that this makes a comparison with costs easier. Within this approach, there can be a tendency to focus on the benefits that can be easily quantified and converted into monetary values and to ignore elements that are more difficult to quantify. However, there have been attempts to expand the approach by monetising 'nature' or natural elements in order to include them in an economic analysis. In this approach 'nature' is seen as a stock of capital from which benefits flow (see Dasgupta, 2021). As Imrie (2021) points out, this is meant to identify and account for the stock of renewable and non-renewable resources in the natural world in order to provide the basis for informed judgements about how human actions impact on the quality and quantity of natural resources. For example, using this approach, if the services of forest elephants were valued as much more than the price gained by poachers, this would justify action to prevent poaching. If the services to humans were viewed as less than this, then no action would be justified. This is a controversial approach and there is considerable disquiet over the financial characterisation of the natural world, seeing it as an anthropocentric understanding of ecosystems and organisms as capital that derive value from how well they 'serve' humanity. 'Instead of appreciating things in their own right, we relegate them to the objectlessness of standing reserve' to be of potential use by humans (Von Maltzahn, 1994: 43). *Guardian* writer George Monbiot (2018) calls the approach 'morally wrong, intellectually vacuous, emotionally alienating and self-defeating'. He argues that:

> Unless something is redeemable for money, a pound or dollar sign placed in front of it is senseless: price represents an expectation of payment, in accordance with market rates. In pricing a river, a landscape or an ecosystem, either you are lining it up for sale, in which case the exercise is sinister, or you are not, in which case it is meaningless. (Monbiot, 2018)

Monbiot concludes that: 'The notions that nature exists to serve us; that its value consists of the instrumental benefits we can extract; that this value can be measured in cash terms; and that what can't be measured does not matter, have proved lethal to the rest of life on Earth' (2018).

There are doubts about the accuracy of the financial estimates made and the possibility of incorporating all of the important elements into any financial model, as well as the values incorporated into them and who gets to stipulate these. Clapham and Foye (2019) review common economic assessments of housing outcomes such as house price changes, rent levels and affordability ratios, and draw attention to the value judgements made in them but rarely made explicit. For example, they stress that affordability ratios require judgements on what proportion of income is appropriate to be spent on housing costs and what 'reasonable' standard of housing people should be able to afford. House price indicators hide important issues about who benefits and loses from increases or reductions in prices. The underlying assumptions of the economic approach are identified by Clapham and Foye:

Thus, according to the mainstream economic theory today, individuals have certain preferences – preference for a garden, or detached home – which when met, leads to an increase in happiness. The objective of policy should therefore be to satisfy these preferences insofar as possible – through maximising incomes, reducing the cost of housing etc. – thus producing the greatest happiness for the greatest number. These preferences are revealed through people's behaviour in the marketplace, and therefore the value of something, indeed, anything, is equivalent only to what people are willing to pay for it, and nothing more. If people are willing to pay an extra £1000 per annum to increase their lifespan by six months (through, for instance, paying for better healthcare), and they are also willing to spend an extra £1000 per annum for a spare room, then both of these goods are of equivalent value. (Clapham and Foye, 2019: 11)

The same argument can be applied to Nature such as in the life of elephants or other animals. The major criticism of the economic approach when applied to housing or other aspects of Nature is that it tends to a view of Nature as entirely an economic commodity with the assumption, following Sandel (2012), that it can be priced and traded as in carbon trading schemes around the world (for a critical review see Kedward et al, 2020). If someone in the market is prepared to pay the economic price then an elephant can be killed, because the ethical issues are not given importance in this kind of analysis. Therefore, this approach can be characterised as viewing houses as economic commodities that can be traded in a market rather than emphasising their use value to the residents and the rest of Nature.

The financial impacts of housing and other elements of Nature have rarely been related to the impact on human and animal lives in general through concepts such as wellbeing. For example, as Clapham and Foye (2019) point out, it is not clear that there is a direct relationship between economic gain and subjective wellbeing because people adapt to their situation over time and change their expectations so that increases in the standard of housing may only bring about an increase in happiness for a short time period. Also, people's satisfaction is influenced by the relative comparison with others in their reference group. Therefore, the basic assumptions of the economic model are shown to be problematic and subject to complex factors. Housing is not just an economic good and houses have a value that is not just economic and cannot be measured in financial terms. There is an important argument, that is accepted in this book, that the characterisation and practice of houses being predominantly a commodity used to create or store wealth or value is at the heart of many current housing problems such as problems of housing shortage, affordability and homelessness (for a discussion see, for example, Clapham, 2019). This issue is explored more fully in following chapters of the book. Further, we argue that the conceptualisation of housing as an economic, market good has led to many of the problems that can be identified in the impact that housing arrangements have on the rest of Nature. Therefore, in this book we seek to use a different approach to define the field of housing and to study the impact of housing arrangements on residents and the rest of Nature.

In seeking an answer to the questions of the scope and definition of the field of housing study and policy it is useful to start with the reasons that the state has become involved in housing problems. Governments in many countries have intervened in housing issues because of the impact of poor physical conditions on the health of residents and communities. Early public policy interventions often focused on the physical condition of the houses and its impact on disease (for the example of the UK see Gauldie, 1974). The key issues were considered to be whether dwellings were hygienic or large enough. Did they have clean water or allow for the circulation of fresh air? Were there too many people living there so they were overcrowded and prohibited healthy living? Programmes and policies enacted included public health initiatives to provide clean water and slum clearance of neighbourhoods judged to be most at risk. This was sometimes supplemented by programmes aimed at renovating existing housing or building new, more healthy dwellings. Such programmes have continued in most countries to the present day and the aims of avoiding ill health and promoting good health have been enshrined in mechanisms such as building codes and planning regulations. The focus of these initiatives is usually on the physical or material house rather than on the people living in them. In some of the early examples, slums were cleared without thought about, or provision for, where evicted residents were to be housed in the future. The standards used to judge the need for intervention and to evaluate its usefulness were held to be 'objective' standards of physical condition, or of health and incidence of disease, that could be calculated by professionals and state employees and this was often done without reference to the residents concerned (Dennis, 1972). Success in housing policy could be measured by the number of houses and their physical size and condition and by measures of overcrowding and health. One can characterise this approach as defining and judging housing studies and policy as being about houses.

In housing research and policy, a more recent approach has been to focus on the relationship between people and their houses in the belief that the success of housing policy is a more subjective phenomenon that can differ between individuals. One can characterise this approach as the concern with homes, which does not supersede the focus on houses, but subsumes it. Material house conditions are important, but the key focus in this approach is on how these are experienced and perceived by residents. There is a recognition that home is an important element of life for many people that has implications for personal identity, individual lifestyle and what has been termed ontological security – the feelings of rootedness and security. Savage et al (2005) used the term 'elective belonging' to describe how some people weave their life stories around the places they live in and how they become integral to their sense of self. A focus on home would lead to measuring the scope, aims and success of a housing policy on the impact on people and their lives. A simple indicator of this would be the satisfaction of people with their housing. Recently the debate about the appropriate impact has focused on ideas of subjective wellbeing (for a review see Clapham and Foye, 2019, and further discussion in Chapter 4) where the outcome of a policy is gauged with reference to the subjective views of the people affected by it. This approach has been refined through the application of a framework based on the capabilities approach. From this perspective a housing policy is judged on the basis of the increase in the life capabilities of those affected (Clapham and Foye, 2019; Foye, 2020; Kimhur, 2020). Wellbeing or capability may be influenced by physical housing conditions but there may not be a direct relationship. People may move to a larger house and their wellbeing may not increase in the medium term for a number of factors including a comparison with the housing situation of others or an adaptation to the new circumstances. (For a fuller discussion of the concepts of wellbeing and capability see Chapter 4.)

The focus on homes has two key limitations. One is the concentration on the wellbeing or capabilities of current populations and the neglect of future cohorts. The second limitation, which has brought the lack of a future perspective into sharp relief, is the lack of exploration of factors outside the dwelling that include the relationship between house, homes and other elements of Nature.

To overcome the two drawbacks of the focus on home and wellbeing in defining the scope of housing research and policy, the concept of sustainability may be used to increase the time frame to include future generations as well as widening the analysis to include other aspects of Nature. However, the use of sustainability as a foundational concept has a number of drawbacks. First, the term has been widely used and has been broadened to include social and economic as well as ecological concerns, and it can be argued that this makes the term very difficult to define in any useful sense. For example, what should the timescale be? What balance should there be between the ecological and other factors? How should Nature be defined and what factors should this include? It may be argued that these issues could be overcome by adopting a very specific definition of the term, but there are two crucial drawbacks. The first is that there is no specific language or framework to link the animal, material and human elements of Nature together, and we will engage with this more fully in later chapters. The second is that the framework focuses on the human element. The definition usually made defines the focus as the sustainability of human populations and only includes other elements of Nature if it impacts on humans. Is it an acceptable outcome if humans survive but almost all other biological forms except those that humans rely on for food or other sustenance are wiped out? Therefore, what is needed is a framework that uses a common language to discuss the relationship between humans and other aspects of Nature and does not exclusively focus on human sustainability. Wilber notes that the study of what he terms the ecological crisis through recent approaches (what we will term in Chapter 2 new materialism) has identified this issue and criticises existing narrow approaches that are primarily human-centred:

> These approaches further maintain that the only way we can heal the planet, and heal ourselves, is by replacing this fractured worldview with a worldview that is more holistic, more relational, more integrative, more Earth-honoring and less arrogantly human-centred. A worldview, in short, that honors the entire web of life, a web that has intrinsic value in and of itself, but a web that, not incidentally, is the bone and marrow of our own existence as well. (Wilber, 2000: 12)

In summary, it is argued here that researchers and policy makers in housing need to adopt a wider concept of housing that sees it as part of Nature. This requires three important elements. The first is a definition of the field and a foundational concept that incorporates the human, material and animal elements of Nature. The concept advocated here is that of 'inhabitation', which will be discussed in the next section. The second element is a theoretical framework that can incorporate all of these elements and provide the basis for the suite of research methodologies and techniques necessary to investigate the issues involved. Here, the practices approach is advocated, which is discussed more fully in the following two chapters. The third element is a method for the evaluation of housing outcomes that includes all of the human, material and animal elements. This is discussed in Chapter 4, which proposes a suite of concepts built around ideas of capabilities and wellbeing that can be applied to all elements of Nature.

Dwelling and inhabitation

What language can we use to define the field of study that is already inclusive of the dwelling structure itself, the inhabitants of the structure, and the outside or context of that structure that respects its role as part of Nature? The word 'house' refers to the structure that provides people with shelter or a place to dwell, and in the abstract, refers also to the people or family living in a building as the household (what the building holds). Therefore, the word 'house' ignores the material and animal context in which the building is located. House either refers to a physical structure or (when used in the term household) points to a collective term for those making themselves comfortable inside or finding protection inside a building against what is outside, separating or sheltering themselves from the elements. The word 'home' is similarly defined, including also being defined as the physical structure and those occupying it as well as also referring to an environment offering security and happiness, which is an affective term for how one feels about a place, referring to the relation between the person and the *place*, rather than a term referring to a collective of living entities and Nature.

Two alternative terms have received some prominence in recent thought on this topic. Following the work of Heidegger, the terms 'dwelling' and 'inhabitation' have been used. Lancione (2020) defines the verb form of the term dwelling as 'our way of being and becoming into the world' and argues that the term 'invites us to ask about the performance of housing, that is, what it does for people'. Lancione also uses the term to examine agency among dwellers and argues that much current housing research focuses on structural theories and neglects the possibility of political change through local action by dwellers, particularly those suffering housing precarity. The most comprehensive and interesting account of dwelling is provided by Ingold (2000). Ingold argues that 'it is through being inhabited, rather than through its assimilation to a formal design specification, that the world becomes a meaningful environment for people. In what follows, I refer to this position as the "dwelling perspective"' (Ingold, 2000: 173). For Ingold, the verb dwelling describes the primary process of living and making sense of the world. Using the example of hunter-gatherers, he argues that 'it is through dwelling in a landscape, through the incorporation of its features into a pattern of everyday activities, that it becomes home' (Ingold, 2000: 57). Adopting Gibson's (1979) view of perception, he sees dwelling as the process of gaining knowledge through daily activity in the world:

> Knowledge of the world is gained by moving about in it, exploring it, attending to it, ever alert to the signs by which it is revealed. Learning to see, then, is a matter not of acquiring schemata for mentally constructing the environment but of acquiring the skills for direct perceptual engagement with its constituents, human and non-human, animate and inanimate. (Ingold, 2000: 55)

Following Gibson, he argues that the world becomes a meaningful place for people through being lived in, rather than through having been constructed along the lines of some formal design. Meanings are not attached by the mind to objects in the world, rather these objects take on their significance – or in Gibson's terms, they afford what they do – by virtue of their incorporation into a characteristic pattern of day-to-day activities. Therefore, meaning is constructed through the relations involved in people's practical engagement with their lived-in environments (Ingold, 2000). In analysing this process of knowledge and skill acquisition Ingold emphasises the importance of everyday practices that make 'home' and one's sense of being in the world. Although Ingold does not use the concept of practices his argument fits very well with it, as is shown later in the book.

Ingold relates his concept of dwelling to the work of Bourdieu and his concept of habitus which is seen not as a mental construct, but as a skill achieved by practical engagement with the world:

> For thinking and feeling, in Bourdieu's account, do not go on in an interior subjective (or intersubjective) space of images and representations but in the space of people's actual engagement in the settings of practical activity. Whereas cultural models are supposed to exist independently of, and prior to, their application in particular situations of use – such as in doing things or making things, or in the interpretation of experience – the habitus exists only as it is instantiated in the activity itself. In other words, the habitus is not expressed in practice, it rather subsists in it. (Ingold, 2000: 162)

Bourdieu emphasises the practical mastery that we associate with skill – a mastery that is carried in our bodies and not just in our heads and is gained through routinely carrying out specific tasks involving characteristic postures and gestures, or what Bourdieu calls a particular body hexis. '"A way of walking, a tilt of the head, facial expressions, ways of sitting and of using implements" – all of these, and more, comprise what it takes to be an accomplished practitioner, and together they furnish a person with his or her bearings in the world' (Bourdieu, 1977: 87).

Roth (2018) also sees dwelling as an active process that makes our place in the world. 'Being means dwelling in a world. There is no world apart from our dwelling' (Roth, 2018: 16). The concept of dwelling 'emphasizes being in and inhabiting a world that is not distinct from us' (Roth, 2018: 25).

> Dwelling therefore captures many characteristics of the human form of being. In our everyday experience, that is, in what we live and live through, building and thinking, as dwelling, are habitual and arise from the fact that we inhabit the earth. This earth is the reference point for who we are and what we think: it is the reference point for our animate bodies and living things so that we may recognize one another as different from thing-bodies; the earth given to (not constructed by) all of us in the same mode, therefore, is the ground for solidarity. The places we inhabit lead to habits, habitual practices, and habitus, sets of structured structuring dispositions that ground the homology between

human ways of being and their natural and social environments. Habitus fits us like the habits we wear. (Roth, 2018: 28)

Although Roth (2018) uses the term dwelling for the active process he is describing, he also recognises similar related terms:

Dwelling (in/habiting) immediately grounds this approach to knowing and learning in the environment because sociologically, the now archaic term habiting (dwelling, abiding, residing, and sojourning) not only implies habitus (structured, structuring dispositions), habits, inhabitation, and habitat but also labor, the body, and consciousness. That is, dwelling leads us to a practical foundation of being and becoming, where building and thinking are shaped by an ex post facto awareness of dwelling. (Roth, 2018: 18)

Boano and Astolfo (2020) prefer the term inhabitation to that of dwelling. Although the term dwelling can be effectively and appropriately used and the choice is a largely personal one, the term 'inhabitation' is preferred here as it includes the positive aspect of 'dwelling' but has other dimensions that meet the needs explored in the book. The term inhabitation is in common usage and as a verb can be defined as: to live in (a place), as people or animals; or to exist or be situated within. We define inhabitation here as the process of living in a place. As the concept of home subsumes but also transcends the concept of house, so the concept of inhabitation subsumes and transcends both house and home to include the situation or context in which the activities of living are undertaken.

The concept of inhabitation has a number of useful elements which help to flesh out this simple definition. First, the concept is grounded in the idea of living in a place, but this is only sketchily defined, which suits our purposes here. In most societies the primary place of inhabitation for humans can be taken as an individual dwelling (or house and home) and so this is the primary focus in this book. But some meanings of the related term habitation refer to a colony or settlement or community setting and this is a good recognition that there are very strong links between what happens in a house and what occurs outside the home and this is reflected in the discussion in Chapter 7 of inhabitation practices that take place outside the home but are closely linked to it. Therefore, the concept can be used at different geographical scales according to the issue under consideration and the particular research or policy focus. This enables the concept to be flexible and adaptable to specific circumstances. Also, unlike the term dwelling, the place does not imply a fixed building (a dwelling as a noun) as it may be a nest, a den, a shop doorway, a park bench or a bivouac as well as a house. This means the term is applicable to different forms of fixed abode for people and animals as well as to places that are inhabited without the existence of a building. The term inhabitation can be used in all these contexts, although it is recognised that the practices involved may vary widely according to the individual circumstances. Rather than categorising situations at the outset, it is preferable to derive them from empirical inquiry.

Second, the term has been applied to both humans and animals and so foregrounds the links between them. As was argued earlier, any dwelling is the place of living for some humans and some animals, whether these are pets or other (perhaps unwelcome) animals such as spiders or mice, and is the home of millions of simple living organisms such as viruses and bacteria. The term inhabitation (and its related term of habitation) is often used with the prefix of 'co-' to reflect the idea that living is undertaken with other species. In other words, there are overlapping inhabitations occurring in any house or place.

Third, the term shares a root with the term habitat that refers to the natural environment of an organism or the place that is natural for the life and growth of an organism and so highlights the importance of the environment or context of inhabitation. As argued by Ingold (2000) and Roth (2018), living in any place involves interaction with the outside human, material and animal phenomena. These may be a threat to valued activities of everyday life (as in the bushfire or COVID-19 examples) or may be valued opportunities to walk in forests or green places or to grow vegetables or flowers. Either way, they impact strongly on the activity of living and should be included in any analysis of living arrangements as the use of the concept of inhabitation emphasises.

Fourth, the term shares a common root with the term habitable, which is often used to define houses that are above a minimum physical standard. This link helps to underline the importance of any standard being based on the lifestyles of the occupants and their perception and use of the property, in other words on their inhabitation practices.

Fifth, the concept of inhabitation relates to the sociological term habitus used by Bourdieu as a way of bringing together the structural and agency elements of human action. Lancione (2020) and Boano and Astolfo (2020) argued that the terms dwelling or inhabitation were emancipatory in that they emphasised individual and community agency through social practices that could bring about change, whereas much previous research focused primarily on the structures that were presumed to be the primary influencing force. The concept of inhabitation places emphasis on the practices of living (including the contextual interactions discussed in this chapter) and sees them as the product of the interaction between agency and structure. The concept of practices brings these elements together and forms the basis of the analysis in this book. In the practices approach, the individual is seen as a carrier of practices that are made up of a number of elements such as materials, meaning and competence (Shove et al, 2012). Living practices differ between individual households depending on personal choice and lifestyle, but there are patterns that are structured by powerful forces in society that may include the house-building industry, land-use planning regulations, environmental regulation and so on. Therefore, the concept of inhabitation places emphasis on the living practices involved in a place and the individual and structural forces that influence these. The concept of practices is an important analytical tool that can form the basis of an examination of inhabitation and this is explored in depth in Chapter 3. The term 'social practice' is often used in the literature but this seems too narrow as a practice involves many factors other than the 'social' whether it be economic or other human concerns or material or animal elements. Therefore, the general term 'practice' is used here to mean a routinised type of behaviour that consists of several elements interconnected to one another, such as meanings, competencies and materials.

The use and definition of the term inhabitation is not enough by itself to provide a useful guide for research and policy as the concept needs to be fleshed out in more detail. As the concern here is with the practices that are involved in living in a place such as a house and home or the process of inhabitation, the concept of 'inhabitation practices' is used to capture this. This concept will be examined further in the following chapters and forms the cornerstone of the analysis presented in the book.

Outline of the book

This chapter has drawn out the links between housing and the animal and material world that are important if housing is to play its part in moves towards a better relationship between people and the rest of Nature. It has covered the first two propositions outlined in the introduction, which are the need to see houses and their occupants as part of Nature and not divorced from it, and the adoption of the concept of inhabitation to guide analysis. However, the analysis has been on a very general level and little detail has been given on the analytical tools to be used or the suggested mode and scope of analysis which form the basis of the third and fourth propositions outlined earlier. Therefore, the argument in the book proceeds with an examination of the strengths and weaknesses of existing approaches used to examine these issues before proceeding to provide more detail on the proposed way forward. Chapter 2 begins the task of constructing an appropriate conceptual framework to study the processes and state of inhabitation by examining existing approaches that have been termed 'new materialism' that attempt to provide a way of linking analysis of human and non-human phenomena. Examples that have been advocated for housing studies are actor-network theory (ANT) and assemblage. Despite their popularity in much academic discourse, these approaches have not been widely adopted in housing studies and have not been incorporated into the mainstream of housing research and policy. The chapter describes the approaches and searches for reasons for their lack of impact. The discussion highlights the strengths of the approaches, but argues that they need to be developed and applied to the particular circumstances of housing or inhabitation. The argument here is that networks and assemblages are not complete theories by themselves, but alternatively can be used as sensitivities to the issues involved in analysis of inhabitation and provide a general framework for a more detailed analysis of inhabitation practices. Chapter 3 builds on this discussion to develop the concept of inhabitation practices as the basis of an approach that draws on new materialism but which overcomes some of its weaknesses. The chapter builds on the existing concept of social practices and offers a discussion of the strengths and weaknesses of the approach and its suitability for the analysis of inhabitation. Chapter 4 examines some of the issues involved in turning this general approach into a practicable and viable research method. It discusses the need for a common language and a more holistic approach in housing policy, practice and research that can guide the formulation of the concept of inhabitation practices. The chapter also discusses the techniques that are useful for the evaluation of housing policies and programmes that consider the wide scope of factors that are identified here. Chapters 5, 6 and 7 continue with some examples of these practices and their impact. Chapter 5 examines the inhabitation practices involved in the consumption of housing or living in a space. Chapter 6 explores the issues involved in the practices of housing production and the discourses that underpin them. Chapter 7 analyses the practices involved in the spatial context of the dwelling, whether it is sited in a city or the countryside. Chapter 8 concludes by summarising the key themes of the book and charting a way forward for housing research and policy.

Conclusion

The case has been made for the need to view houses and their inhabitants as part of Nature rather than being divorced from it and to adopt the concept of inhabitation to define the scope and form of the analysis required. However, the sceptical reader is likely to ask what relevance this has to housing research and the making of housing policy. The COVID-19 and climate change aspects have been previously mentioned, but as well as a concern with the headline environmental issues, an understanding of the links between the human, material and animal elements of inhabitation are relevant for more traditional housing issues. Many examples will be given in the Chapters 5, 6 and 7 but the general point can be made with a few specific issues. For example, a person with a pet dog may be denied access to homeless accommodation. Some people may consider the comfort of pets as an important element in their housing choices. Therefore, the contention in the book is that an understanding of the interaction between the three elements is pivotal for an understanding of the housing situation and for housing policy.

The approach advocated here stimulates a different focus on the elements of housing inequality and a wider discussion of the elements of disadvantage in housing. How do inhabitation practices change depending on housing circumstances? What kinds of disadvantage do some people experience and how does it impact on wider aspects of their lives? How does homelessness affect the inhabitation practices of everyday life? How does housing disadvantage link to wider issues such as climate change and material use? For example, it may be that inequality means an increased demand for housing space by affluent people and by others trying to achieve a perceived minimum standard with an increased impact on material use and climate change.

The argument in this section is that an expanded view of housing that sees it as inhabitation opens up important questions of policy and practice and the factors that influence them. The scope of analysis is widened to incorporate material and animal elements which can add to the understanding of the impacts on many aspects of human life and on other species. A lack of concern with climate change in housing as in other fields may lead to more bushfires that increase housing insecurity. At a very different level, the lack of a view of a garden or the inability to keep a pet may reduce the wellbeing and self-esteem of a vulnerable resident. These and many other examples given in later chapters show that the concern with the material and animal elements of inhabitation practices is not a peripheral concern, but is central to many of the issues that have dominated housing research and policy over a sustained period of time.

2

New materialism in housing studies: opportunities and obstacles

In 1992 Jim Kemeny made an influential plea for housing studies to be more theoretically aware through the application of theories from the mainstream social disciplines. In his own work, Kemeny drew on social constructionism as his theoretical framework and applied it to the study of housing tenures and to international comparative research (Kemeny and Lowe, 1998). The framework became popular in housing studies and an edited collection in 2004 (Jacobs et al, 2004) showed the scope of the research that had been undertaken under its rubric. However, there has been an increasing dissatisfaction with the constraints and lacunae in the underlying tenets of social constructionism and it has been challenged by a number of important developments and trends in social theory and research such as materialism and practice theory.

It may appear strange to start a chapter on new materialism with a discussion of social constructionism, but the latter's popularity in housing studies and the links between the two approaches make this way of proceeding useful. In part, new materialism was adopted as a reaction to the social constructionist approach in the social sciences. In addition, the following chapter will outline the practice approach that is adopted in this book and it is useful to see this in relation to both social constructionism and new materialism as there are some features that are related to both approaches. It is argued that the practice approach provides a more holistic framework by integrating the strengths of the other two and overcomes some of their drawbacks.

Therefore, this chapter begins with a brief description of social constructionism and its impact on academic housing research and policy and practice. The strengths and weaknesses of the approach are outlined and the increasingly popular alternative of new materialism that builds on the weaknesses is considered. New materialism overcomes the relative neglect of material elements in social constructionism, which was dominated by the study of language and discourse.

The chapter covers just two of the many possible approaches that have been applied to housing given its multidisciplinarity. The two theories examined here stem from sociology and human geography and have been chosen because of my familiarity with these areas as well as their popularity in the housing field. However, as outlined in the Preface, the choice is a very personal one that reflects my own academic journey in search of knowledge in the housing field. Therefore, the choice reflects how I have come to take the current position that is reflected in the rest of the book.

What is social constructionism?

There have been a number of reviews of social constructionism as it has been applied in housing (Jacobs and Manzi, 2000; Jacobs et al, 2004; Clapham, 2012). Jacobs et al (2004) emphasise its roots in discourse analysis, symbolic interactionism, studies of social problems and policy narratives, and the sociology of power. Clapham (2012) sees the roots of social constructionism in the traditions of symbolic interactionism, phenomenology, ethnomethodology and postmodernism. Travers (2004) highlights the many debates within social constructionist approaches, but argues that housing researchers have tended to ignore these and focus instead on pursuing a relatively superficial and empirically oriented path. As Travers (2004: 27) argues, 'it is in practice easy to combine different epistemological assumptions, or shift between different theories when conducting a piece of sociological analysis'. Most housing researchers have based their approach on the writings of Berger and Luckmann (1967), who were responsible for popularising the approach and providing a useful way forward that tended to hide the underlying tensions. For example, Travers (2004) argues that their work is an amalgamation of the relativism of Schutz (1967) with the objectivism of Parsons (1938) and is an example of the dichotomy that has haunted social constructionist research and encouraged a split between so-called weak and strong constructionism depending on the extent to which researchers feel able to take their relativism.

Despite the debates and disagreements between individual writers and researchers in the social constructionist tradition, there are a number of commonalities that most would agree are the basic tenets of a social constructionist approach. Berger and Luckmann (1967) state that the fundamental tenet is that social life is constructed by people through interaction. It is through interaction that individuals define themselves and the world they inhabit and so it is through interaction that the nature of individuals becomes apparent to themselves and others. Therefore, within social constructionism there is an emphasis on face-to-face interaction where an individual's subjectivity becomes available to themselves and others through what they say and their body language. Language, seen as a system of vocal signs, is the way that interaction can be extended to include non-face-to-face encounters. As Berger and Luckmann argue:

> Language is capable not only of constructing symbols that are highly abstracted from everyday experience, but also of bringing back these symbols and presenting them as objectively real elements in everyday

life. In this manner, symbolism and symbolic language become essential constituents of the reality of everyday life and the common-sense apprehension of this reality. I live in a world of signs and symbols every day. (Berger and Luckmann, 1967: 40–41)

These common-sense systems of meaning, or discourses, describe the nature of the world, or reality, and become taken for granted as an objective reality that is above the subjectivity of individuals. They can be transmitted from generation to generation through processes of socialisation and can be institutionalised into codes of conduct that define and construct appropriate behaviour. Therefore, the focus in social constructionism is on the linguistic and social construction of reality and the interpretation and negotiation of the meaning of the lived world.

As mentioned earlier, social constructionism is an amalgam of different research traditions such as symbolic interactionism and phenomenology but, subsequently, it has been developed by postmodern writers such as Foucault (1972), Bauman (1992) and Giddens (1984). None of these authors would regard themselves as social constructionists, but their work has been used and adapted to supplement the basic tenets of social constructionism by those wishing to overcome some of the disadvantages and shortcomings of the approach. An example in the field of housing is the housing pathways approach (Clapham, 2002) that is grounded in social constructionism, but adds the structuration theory of Giddens to broaden the perspective.

Social constructionism has made a considerable contribution to housing studies in a number of fields. In terms of research method, the focus on language and its consolidation into discourses has meant that much research in this tradition has used discourse analysis or critical discourse analysis as its research technique. In terms of topics, Kemeny's (1992) writing on the social construction of tenure was important in unpicking the meaning of tenure categories and the way they were constructed. This has been followed up by analyses of government documents as well as common understandings of tenure by authors such as Gurney (1999). Other research has focused on the construction of social problems such as homelessness (for example, Jacobs et al, 1999). This work has shown that such problems are perceived to not have objective foundations but are 'constructed on shifting sands of public rhetoric, coalition building, interest group lobbying and political expediency' (Jacobs et al, 2004: 5). The social constructionist approach led to the policy process being examined through discourse analysis of policy statements and documents. A third and less developed focus on housing research was on the interactions that shaped the construction process. In the case of policymaking the study of policy documents was supplemented with an analysis of the way that powerful interest groups were able to set the policy agenda through their actions. Other examples are Clapham et al's (2000) and Darcy and Manzi's (2004) work on housing management. These studies used a discourse analysis of policy statements and procedures but also studied the interaction between housing officers and tenants. This approach added an important critical dimension to traditional political science approaches to policymaking but lacked a sufficient focus on power in shaping discourse and other outcomes.

Social constructionism was also deployed by Kemeny (Kemeny and Lowe, 1998) and others to compare housing policies and outcomes between different countries using the welfare regimes paradigm that saw policy as an outcome of socially constructed welfare regimes that were shaped by political forces such as the relative power of labour and capital in national politics. This approach helped move the comparative study of housing policies away from descriptive or evolutionary perspectives that had dominated previous studies (for example, Donnison, 1967).

The social constructionist approach gave an important impetus to housing research by providing a theoretical framework that helped to counterpoint the largely descriptive, positivist and policy-oriented studies that had previously predominated. Nevertheless, there were many drawbacks and constraints.

A long-standing debate in social constructionism has centred on the extent of its subjectivity. If reality is a social construction then a social constructionist analysis is also a social construction. It is contradictory to criticise the perceived objectivity of discourses that are being examined while extolling the critique as being objective and truthful. One reaction to this problem is to admit that a social constructionist researcher's interpretation of events is also subjective, but given the lack of a believable way of choosing between different interpretations, this undermines the value of the approach and hinders its use in the policymaking process if policy makers are looking for more definite outcomes and policy proposals (see Clapham, 2018). In the housing research field, which had many links to policy and practice organisations, the value of the approach became questioned as it focused more on critiquing existing policies rather than suggesting alternatives that could be readily implemented.

Another major criticism of social constructionism focused on the assumption that individuals only achieve their humanity through social interaction. This approach tended to downgrade individual differences and genetic and psychological dispositions and the embodied nature of human thought and actions (see Shilling, 2003). A key question is how our emotions and bodily feelings relate to discourse and shape meaning. This may be important in considering issues important to housing studies such as the meaning that homes have for us that may contain elements of all these factors.

The importance given in the approach to language and meaning can lead to a position that the relationship between humans and the material world is seen entirely in this light. In other words, the reality of material phenomena is constructed through their meaning to humans. This position does not necessarily deny an 'objective' reality of materials, but sees the importance to social science as being the impact this has on humans through the meaning they give to it. Material reality is mediated by social constructs. But even if it is accepted that there is an objective material reality, social constructionism offers no clues as to how it can be investigated, leaving this to other disciplines and approaches, and so limits the analysis of the effects of material changes. For example, the impact of computers and other information technologies on human life and practices cannot be reducible just to the meaning they hold, but also to the possibilities and constraints that the material technology makes available. The material world is considered only as a passive conductor of meaning and the physical properties that material objects have and the influence this has on the way that humans can use them and exercise agency are neglected. An extension of this is that animals are not considered as agents or actors as they do not, in general, possess language.

Many of these criticisms have been brought to the fore by what has been termed the material turn in social science (whereas social constructionism can be said to be part of the earlier linguistic turn) and the implications of this are now considered. Maller (2018) includes social constructionism in what she categorises as representational theories where knowledge is created through accurate subjective, textual or linguistic 're-presentations' of the world that separate language and text from materials and materiality, and discount dynamic relations between agents. It is clear that these features of social constructionism contradict the ideas of Ingold (2000) and others on the concept of dwelling outlined in the previous chapter and which have been adopted in the conception of inhabitation which forms the cornerstone of this book. Ingold (2000) criticises the emphasis in social constructionism on the mind viewed as separate from the body and uses the perceptual theories of Gibson (1979) outlined in the previous chapter to challenge this view:

> The mind, then, was conceived as a kind of data-processing device, akin to a digital computer, and the problem for the psychologist was to figure out how it worked. But Gibson's approach was quite different. It was to throw out the idea, that has been with us since the time of Descartes, of the mind as a distinct organ that is capable of operating upon the bodily data of sense. Perception, Gibson argued, is not the achievement of a mind in a body, but of the organism as a whole in its environment, and is tantamount to the organism's own exploratory movement through the world. If mind is anywhere, then, it is not 'inside the head' rather than 'out there' in the world. To the contrary, it is immanent in the network of sensory pathways that are set up by virtue of the perceiver's immersion in his or her environment. (Ingold, 2000: 2–3)

This view of perception leads Ingold to question ideas of cultural impacts on behaviour through representational discourses and language and to assert the importance of the acquisition of knowledge and skills from one generation to the next through learning during the process of living in the environment:

> Throughout this history, the assumption has persisted that people construct the world, or what for them is 'reality', by organising the data of sensory perception in terms of received and culturally specific conceptual schemata. But in recent anthropology, this assumption has been challenged by advocates of 'practice theory', who argue that cultural knowledge, rather than being imported into the settings of practical activity, is constituted within these settings through the development of specific dispositions and sensibilities that lead people to orient themselves in relation to their environment and to attend to its features in the particular ways that they do. (Ingold, 2000: 153)

Attempts to overcome the drawbacks of social constructionism have included 'non-representational' theories that focus on materiality, performativity and affect, and attempt to include non-humans in their scope, focus on (bodily) action and interaction, and overcome the mind/body dichotomy in much theory by stressing the embodied and emotional elements of human (and animal) feeling and action. There is not the space to cover all of these theories here (for a relevant review see Maller, 2018) and so the focus is on the theories labelled 'new materialism' that are most relevant to the argument here. Practice theories mentioned by Ingold and adopted in this book are reviewed in the following chapter.

New materialism

There is no accepted definition of new materialism, but Maller (2018: 47) uses the term to describe theories that 'orient themselves around the physical affects, liveliness and agency of living and non-living matter at various scales and forms, from the micro of sub-atomic particles to bodies and complex urban assemblages such as cities'. There is no generally accepted list of the approaches that are considered to lie within the new materialist banner. Gabriel and Jacobs (2008) included approaches such as ANT and new materialism in their discussion of what they labelled the post-social turn and it would be appropriate to include here the assemblage approach, which has been influential in current social science thinking. Each of these approaches has its own traditions and advocates, but it is difficult to draw a clear line between ANT, new materialism and assemblages with differences between them seeming to be dwarfed by disagreements within the individual approaches. Also, there seems to be no generally acceptable definition or way of working in individual traditions. For example, the contrasts between the approaches of DeLanda (2002) and Latour (1993) are considerable, although there are many areas on which there is agreement. Both use terminology such as networks and assemblages, but their theoretical and empirical assumptions and definitions are very different. Therefore, any review is faced with a bewildering variety of approaches. For ease of exposition the overall term new materialism is used here to cover the field where the basic approach is described and the major areas of agreement and disagreement are outlined.

Gabriel and Jacobs (2008) make the point that those they name post-social writers (or new materialists as labelled here) do not privilege the linguistic (as in much social constructionist research), but rather they recognise, quoting Latour, that the socio-technological networks that they trace and describe are 'simultaneously real, like nature, narrated, like discourse, and collective, like society' (Latour, 1993: 6). As Latour explains:

> The ozone hole is too social and too narrated to be truly natural; the strategy of industrial firms and heads of state is too full of chemical reactions to be reduced to power and interest; the discourse of the ecosphere is too real and too social to boil down to meaning effects. (Latour, 1993: 6)

The eclecticism advocated by Latour cuts across many previous traditions in housing studies that have adopted 'social constructionist' or other approaches that are often seen as competing and incompatible paradigms. New materialism seems to offer a way of combining insights from these traditions into a more holistic approach that adopts insights from social constructionism while adding new dimensions.

The basic approach of assemblage theory, which seems to be accepted by many authors of ANT and new materialism, is specified by Storper and Scott:

> Assemblage theory is first and foremost an ontological view of the world conceived as a mass of rhizomatic networks or finely-grained relationships constituting the fundamental character of reality. These networks bind together unique human and non-human objects within fluid, hybrid mosaics forming more or less temporarily stabilised systems of interconnections representing the current state of the observable world. Assemblages become stabilised by 'territorialization' (as opposed to destabilising deterritorialisation) when they are anchored to particular tracts of geographical space. Importantly, any state of reality in this theory is taken to be 'flat' in the sense that any perceived hierarchical or scalar ordering (from a top to a bottom) decomposes back again into the kaleidoscopic, rhizomatic and horizontal relations

that are said to constitute it (DeLanda, 2002; see also Marston et al., 2005). (Storper and Scott, 2016: 1125)

The first tenet common to different versions of new materialism is the acceptance of the agency of material or non-human agents or actants (to use the terminology of ANT and assemblage). Although there are disagreements at the margins of the extent of this agency, it is a key element of the approaches. Gabriel and Jacobs argue that new materialist writers have stressed the need to decentre the human subject as the nucleus of social life and have called for greater recognition of non-human actors (for example, animals, technology and material artefacts) within social scientific inquiry. Assemblage thinking has pioneered the analysis of the significant agency of nonhuman material actants, from buildings and building materials to infrastructural grids and weather systems. Maller (2018) characterises new materialist approaches as seeing matter as 'vibrant' (following Bennett, 2010), that is possessing agency and the capacity to create effects in the world. In this formulation, agency is widely distributed to a range of entities and processes and is not just the preserve of humans, although a differentiation in the nature of different forms of agency is usually made, in other words material agency is not considered to be of the same kind or extent as human agency.

The ascription of agency to material objects has been criticised (Storper and Scott, 2016) as placing humans and material objects on an even footing and having 'a perilous tendency to fail to distinguish between the inanimate character of material objects and the intentionality of humans'. But the criticism seems misplaced as the approach recognises the different forms that agency can take, as we will discuss in more detail in the following chapter.

The second common tenet is the importance of interconnections, whether termed networks or assemblages. Li (2007: 266) usefully defines assemblage as a 'gathering of heterogeneous elements consistently drawn together as an identifiable terrain of action and debate'. These elements include arrangements of humans, materials, technologies, organisations, techniques, procedures, norms and events, all of which have the capacity for agency within and beyond the assemblage. Latour (2005: 238) argues that: 'Things, quasi-objects and attachments are the real centre of the social world not agent, person, member, or participant – nor is it society or its avatars.' McFarlane sums up the position:

[U]rban actors, forms or processes are defined less by a pre-given property and more by the assemblages they enter and reconstitute. The individual elements define the assemblage by their co-functioning, and can be stabilised (territorialised or reterritorialised) or destabilised (deterritorialised) through this mutual imbrication. But this is not to say that an assemblage is a direct result of the properties of its component parts. It is the *interactions* between human and nonhuman components that form the assemblage—interaction as mutually constitutive symbiosis rather than just parts that are related—and these interactions cannot be reduced to individual properties alone. As a form of spatial relationality, assemblage thinking is attentive to both the individual elements *and* the agency of the interactive whole, where the agency of both can change over time and through interactions. (McFarlane, 2011: 208, original emphasis)

As Baker and McGuirk (2017: 4) point out, a further area of agreement is that the new materialist approaches emphasise 'the active composition of networks or assemblages – fitting, connecting, combining, and aligning relations between heterogeneous elements within and across space – the popularity of assemblage results in large part from its understanding of the social as materially heterogeneous, practice-based, emergent and processual'. Latour (2013) stresses the importance of examining the process of construction and maintenance of networks as it is here that important actants and key interactions become visible. McFarlane (2011) argues that a study of the practical, processual aspects of housing is useful for the development of assemblage theory as it provides a way for thinking through how assemblage actually takes place.

Some issues in new materialism

Gabriel and Jacobs (2008) discuss three major criticisms that have previously been directed at new materialism and which they see as obstacles to its adoption in housing studies: (1) that such an approach is insufficiently scientific in that it remains at the level of description and defies grand theorising; (2) that its proponents extend agency to non-humans and thereby insist on the equal analytical treatment of objects and people; and (3) that post-social accounts are politically conservative and fail to change and improve society. The second category is discussed more fully in Chapter 3 and so is not covered in detail here. However, the position taken is that the extension of agency is a very positive move that helps to achieve the purposes of this book. Also, the inclusion of non-human actors does not mean that their agency is viewed as the same as humans in extent or nature. Most versions of new materialism stress that agency is primarily the result of interactions between the individual elements rather than in the characteristics of the individual elements themselves, although as McFarlane (2011) argued, and as we shall see later, we argue for a combination of these approaches. The other two elements of the schema are adopted here, but the scope of the critiques and the challenges they pose for housing research is widened to include other factors not discussed by Gabriel and Jacobs (2008).

Lack of theory

The focus on networks and interactions has been criticised by Storper and Scott (2016: 1126) as leading to 'a descriptive, anecdotal and notably indiscriminate approach to urban investigation'. They criticise what they see as the 'inductive empiricism' and naive objectivism of the approach, and point to its failure to distinguish between the significant and the insignificant in urban analysis. Without theoretical guideposts, Storper and Scott argue that it is no way of teasing out significant relationships or distinguishing between the trivial and the important:

> This mode of analysis presupposes that the 'facts'—in this case, those of interconnection among human and nonhuman actants—speak for themselves rather than requiring mediation or at least animation through theoretical assumptions and interpretive schemata. Thus, in the flattened world of assemblage theory there is a perilous tendency to fail to distinguish between the inanimate character of material objects and the intentionality of humans, and to compound this oversight by under-theorised presentations of social interconnectivity (cf. Tonkiss, 2011). This flattening of the world also evacuates any meaningful political content from assemblage theory since everything is equally important (or equally trivial and unimportant). (Storper and Scott, 2016: 1126)

In many studies using the assemblage concept, there is little theoretical framing and the approach has been used just to provide a justification for an empirical focus on linkages and the relationship between humans and the material world.

Gabriel and Jacobs argue that the claims of post-social (or new materialist) writers are

> extremely modest, relating as they do to the capacity of social science to produce some unanticipated effects or put another way to spotlight the way in which actors and networks are assembling and reassembling. This incremental, contingent and descriptive view of social science presents real challenges for applied housing researchers who favour generalization as a basis for comparison and cumulative knowledge. (Gabriel and Jacobs, 2008: 535)

The discussion has led Baker and McGuirk to conclude that:

> Actor network theory is not a theory. At least, that is what some main exponents have started to suggest (Latour 1999; Law 1999). If it were a theory, it would provide a fixed way of approaching the world,

which would be little better than the reductionist models it sought to replace. Rather it is a general attitude and an attempt to be sensitive to the multitudes of circulating forces that surround us, affecting both each other and ourselves (Latour 1999). It is a way of keeping in mind a range of insights whilst also being ever wary that, if these insights were to solidify into a more defined theory, we would begin denying our own negotiation with the complexity of the world. Under actor network theory, people, objects, plants, animals and ideas all jostle against each other, and it is through these interactions that society takes shape and our understandings of this society find form. (Baker and McGuirk, 2017: 100)

In this understanding, the new materialist approaches are more akin to a research approach than a theoretical framework. For example, Latour recommends that we simply 'follow the actors' (1993) and trace their engagements in whatever ways seem relevant to them. Latour (2005) emphasises the construction of assemblages or networks by human action and implores researchers to get into the interior world of their subjects to understand the construction process and the existence and extent of the assemblages. He argues for a bottom–up and flat ontology with an emphasis on the horizontal links between actors and assemblages.

However, there are differences of emphasis and approach between authors in the tradition. For example, in contrast to the flat ontology of Latour, DeLanda sees assemblages as being the way that universal processes operate 'on the ground' and in specific locations. They are essentially being driven by the 'higher level' processes that define overall directions whereas assemblages constitute the mechanism by which these processes are implemented and amended at a local level. McFarlane illustrates this latter approach through the example of neoliberalism:

One example here is McGuirk and Dowling's argument (2009) that the analytic of assemblage offers one possible route for conceiving neoliberalism not as a universal and coherent project, or even as a generalised hegemonic process characterised by local contingencies, but as a loose collection of urban logics and processes that may or may not structure urban change in different places. They seek to conceive urban change through the lens of 'situated assemblages of different logics, actors, histories, projects and practices that serve not to reify neoliberalism as hegemonic and ascendant, but as one set of possibilities among many. This is an inherently empirical focus, a call to examine practices "on the ground" in a way that remains "open to the practical co-existence of multiple political projects, modes of governance, practices and outcomes generated by and enacted through" specific urban strategies' (McGuirk and Dowling, 2009, p. 177). This is not to underplay the role of neoliberalism, but to focus on the key drivers of inequality on the ground, of which neoliberalism may only be one. (McFarlane, 2011: 209)

As a consequence of the lack of an agreed approach, there is no consistent view of the nature and distribution of power. Some authors such as Latour argue that power resides in the interactions between actants that may vary from situation to situation and so each situation needs to be examined with an open mind. The concept of power is rarely mentioned in his writing and there seems to be little recognition of the structural aspects of power. Latour argues that all relations are reciprocal and symmetrical, which would seem to indicate that he sees power as being widely spread and not related to a few dominant actors. In contrast, DeLanda sees assemblages as a way that power is expressed rather than being its sole source. Other factors such as dominant discourses of neoliberalism can set the context within which networks or assemblages are constructed and function.

The differences within new materialism provide choices for housing researchers. They can simply adopt it as an empirical research method that provides a guide to the research techniques to be employed. However, there are some difficulties in empirical operationalisation of the approach, as we explore in more detail in later chapters. As an illustration, most applications of the assemblage approach in housing have started at the level of the dwelling. The assemblage is constructed by working out from this to examine the linkages that have resulted in the house being what it is in terms of its material form and the social practices that are undertaken within it. In the example of the material forms, the nature of the technologies and their employment needs to be examined. This may involve a questioning of why particular technologies were chosen as well as the organisation of the social practices that influenced the technology chosen and the way it is deployed. Clearly this will involve an analysis of the construction industry. However, the impact of a house is more than this because of the inhabitation practices involved. The house sits in a material landscape of roads, lighting and gardens that is also shared with animals. It is also part of a social landscape that involves the pursuit of a lifestyle that will involve travel to other places, such as work, shopping and leisure activities. The internal and external landscapes will be linked. An 'unsatisfactory' internal situation may lead to a lifestyle that involves lots of time spent outside the home and maybe large expenditures on energy for heating.

To encapsulate all of these linkages is a monumental empirical task even for an individual house. If it is scaled up to the levels of towns or even whole societies the scale of the task is evident. The approach taken in existing studies has been to fill in the broader picture with a number of smaller-scale studies that illuminate part of the picture. The focus of an assemblage does not have to be on a house. In the wider literature examples have been used of 'monsoons' and other phenomena as the focus for the construction of an assemblage. In housing, examples could be taken from particular social practices or material impacts. Previous examples are the use of smart technology, or renewable heating technologies. Examples of social practices could include use of leisure time and the relationship to mobile technologies. The important issue would be to keep in mind the overall picture when constructing what one may call 'mini-assemblages'.

Alternatively, researchers can accept the paradigm as an overall sensibility and import their own theoretical framework into the approach. This may involve adopting the 'flat ontology' of Latour or the more structuralist approach of DeLanda from within the new materialist tradition, or the adoption of other traditions and their adaptation to suit the new sensibility. As will become apparent, this is the approach taken in this book as we use the concept of practices, rooted in theories of structuration, to provide a theoretical framework for new materialism. There is a need for an overarching framework as it is essential to not only focus on the materials themselves but also to consider the political–economic structures and institutions in which they are embedded.

Failure to improve society

Gabriel and Jacobs (2008) reflect a concern that some elements of new materialism (particularly the flat ontology of writers such as Latour) can divert research away from its role in social change and improvement of the condition of human life that has imbued many housing studies. It is certainly the case that much housing research (and many housing researchers) are imbued with an objective of changing housing policy and the housing circumstances of the population as well as understanding and describing existing situations and their causes. One important strand of housing studies can be traced back to the Fabian approach of the pursuit of incremental and progressive social change inherent in the social policy tradition of authors such as Richard Titmuss. At the same time, much research on housing has been funded and directed by government agencies, often set to an agenda situated within dominant political and social discourses of the nature of housing problems. This can lead to an understandable focus on the impact of research on policy priorities which the flat ontology of much new materialist research would find difficult to satisfy. The desired open-endedness of empirical enquiry and the focus on all events highlighted by authors such as Latour would not find favour with many government agencies, research funders or policy focused housing researchers. In addition, the descriptive nature of much new materialist research does not offer the predictive element valued by those looking to take policy action to change a future state of society. In other words, a description of how arrangements are now does not necessarily help with the task of designing a new arrangement that achieves desired outcomes.

The place of social practices

Another important issue with many frameworks and applications of new materialist approaches is the ambivalent position of social practices within the overall assemblage or network. Most definitions include practices along with material and human actants as constituting an assemblage or network. But, as we shall see in Chapter 3, almost all practices involve material and animal as well as human elements. So, a key question is what is included in an assemblage that is not part of a practice? What is the relationship between practices and these other elements? The place of practices is not always clearly articulated in theory or in individual studies, which is important because we will show in the next few chapters that the practice approach overcomes many of the problems with new materialism that have been highlighted here. A foregrounding of practices gives a clear theoretical and empirical focus for research and is easier to apply to policy discussions.

New materialist housing research

In their 2008 paper, Gabriel and Jacobs pointed to research that had adopted this paradigm in housing studies. Gabriel and Jacobs' conclusion was that new materialist (or post-social) accounts can provide a valuable extension to the housing studies project, particularly through a renewed focus on materiality and the modification of a priori analytical frameworks within housing research. It will become evident that the major features of new materialism are very useful in achieving the aims of this book. However, despite a small number of specific studies that have adopted this paradigm there is little evidence of change in dominant approaches in housing studies. The focus in this section is on why change has been so limited. It is argued that the answer is to be found in both the limitations of new materialism and in housing studies itself and its relationship to the policy process. A discussion of these obstacles is necessary if they are to be overcome and the framework is to be developed to provide an appropriate basis for the study of inhabitation.

Gabriel and Jacobs (2008) highlight three areas of housing research where there has been an application of the new materialist approach. The first of these is research on what they term dwelling and domesticity where home can be studied in a way that is sensitive to the relationship between people and materials. Steele and Vizel (2014: 88) illustrate that housing/home is always an assemblage of the human and non-human, where materiality is situated across 'states of being (solid, liquid, gaseous) and elements (air, fire, water and earth)'. When viewed through this approach the world of home swarms with the many socio-technical associations that coproduce home life. Home is not simply the cultivation of a sense of belonging, nor merely a site of consumption, it is quite literally a fabrication. Research in this vein covers a range from studies on the experience of disabled people with the material elements of home (see, for example, Imrie, 1996, 2004) to research on material possessions in the home (see, for example, Miller, 2001) to private gardens (see Hitchings, 2003) as well as domestic animals (see, for example, Franklin, 2006). More recent studies have focused on areas where the link between people and the material elements of home is the most direct and which impacts on environmental goals. For example, assemblage theory has been used in studies of the relationship between humans and the material of the house such as on 'smart homes' (Maalsen, 2020) and energy saving innovations. However, most studies have been confined to the house itself and have not ventured into the outside. They have also been focused on housing consumption rather than its production.

The second area highlighted by Gabriel and Jacobs is the functioning of the housing market. An example here is the work on the performativity of housing markets by Smith et al (2006) who 'are interested in highlighting the complex interplay of human and non-human actors in the creation of local housing markets in order to not only provide a fuller account of markets but also to "inspire a normative debate" about "what they might, one day, become"' (Gabriel and Jacobs, 2008: 95). For Gabriel and Jacobs:

> The post-social approach to housing markets represents a marked shift away from the impulse to view the economy, or rather the market, as an abstract and external force. Instead, researchers are invited to unpack such economic models through close attention to the many actors employed in the process of trading property and buying homes. This performative understanding of markets entails an anthropological practice that can shed light on the intersections between the international world of finance, the taxation regimes of governments, the built form of cities, home building materials and the budgets of households. (Gabriel and Jacobs, 2008: 534)

However, it is fair to say that this approach has not permeated into most work on the economics of housing.

The third area highlighted by Gabriel and Jacobs is neighbourhood planning and housing development. They point to a number of studies that have sought to see the process of planning and housing development using networks and assemblages as the theoretical framework (see, for example, Murdoch, 2000):

These studies provide insight into the constitution of housing policy, neighbourhood planning and the urban form. Not only do they recognize the presence of the non-human, but also how such non-humans actively intervene in and disrupt the order of the city. Moreover, such studies attend to the histories that shape contemporary practices by tracing how 'things' such as government agencies are built up into networks and how these networks are mobilized and stabilized over time. (Gabriel and Jacobs, 2008: 535)

Gabriel and Jacobs (2008) argue that post-social accounts (or new materialism) can provide a valuable extension to the housing studies project, particularly through a renewed focus on materiality and the modification of a priori analytical frameworks within housing research. But the case for this has not been effectively made as the lack of research in this tradition shows. The use of a new materialist framework has been largely confined to those areas in the housing field where the link to material objects is most direct and the approach has not permeated into mainstream housing research or seen its key concepts and approaches widely adopted within this tradition. The examination of some of its weaknesses in the previous section gives some reasons why this has been so and gives urgency for the adoption of a framework that overcomes them.

Conclusion

The existing approaches of new materialism have arguably not made a great impact on housing studies or housing policy even though they may have shed valuable light on specific housing issues as illustrated by the examples cited in the chapter. The main reasons for the limited impact are the difficulties in making an impact on policymaking and the inherent limitations of some versions of the approach. However, these problems are surmountable and in the next two chapters we will start the process of building out from them to provide a more appropriate framework by defining and applying the concept of inhabitation to overcome some of the highlighted barriers. The intention here is to identify the important factors that can be used to act as a foundation for a way forward for housing studies and policy.

A major strength of new materialism is the inclusion of human, animal and material elements in an approach that fits well with the inhabitation concept introduced in the last chapter. The scope of the relationships in networks or assemblages is appropriate for the wide spectrum of relationships and impacts that were identified in the previous chapter and which characterise the field of inhabitation. The use of the term actant to encapsulate that all elements have a capacity to act in conjunction with others is again useful in elucidating the important interconnections between them. In particular, the acceptance in some versions of new materialism that agency exists in the elements singly as well in their interaction is also valuable in teasing out the important factors in generating particular outcomes. However, a major problem of some new materialist approaches is the failure to move beyond the descriptive and to be associated with a theoretical base that enables issues of agency and relative power to be incorporated in the analysis. Therefore, in Chapter 3 the concept of inhabitation practices will be elaborated as a way of overcoming these difficulties and providing a holistic framework that draws on the strengths of new materialism.

One of the identified problems with some new materialist approaches is the failure to find a way of integrating the different elements into a coherent guide for empirical research. In Chapter 4, some ideas of a common research language and holistic method will be explored to better enable diverse elements to be incorporated into a feasible and appropriate empirical approach.

3

Inhabitation practices

In Chapter 1, the first two propositions of the need for a unified view of humans and Nature and the need for the concept of inhabitation were outlined as a basis for devising a framework for the analysis of the interaction between human, animal and material elements that are at the core of the experience and study of house and home or housing policy and research. In Chapter 2, the existing theoretical frameworks of social constructionism and those included under the label of new materialism have been analysed and the obstacles that have hindered their application to housing studies in the past examined. In this chapter it is argued that the strengths of both traditions can be built on by emphasising the concept of social practices and applying it to inhabitation. Therefore, this chapter focuses on the third proposition by expanding on the concept of inhabitation practices as a way of integrating some of the insights generated in previous chapters and providing a focus for analysis. To achieve this, the chapter starts with the concept of social practices, describing its definition and use by different authors and how it has been applied in housing and other fields. This is followed by an examination of the similarities and differences between the new materialist approaches outlined in the previous chapter and social practices. The aim is to find a way forward that integrates the insights from the approaches to provide a conceptual framework for the analysis of inhabitation. The term social practices is used at the outset as this is the term usually used in the literature, however, the adjective social seems limiting when we are here discussing practices that also have animal and material elements. We are also keen to adopt the implication from new materialism and the analysis of the ideas of Wilber in the following chapter that there is no discrete social science and try to move to an approach and terminology that exemplifies the search for a unifying language that includes animal and material as well as human elements. Therefore, as the discussion progresses we will adopt the more general term practices and when we finally relate the concept to our field of enquiry here we will adopt the concept of inhabitation practices.

Social practices

Nicolini (2012) argues that practice theory is not a unified whole, but consists of different ideas pursued by a number of authors. Shove et al (2012) trace the concept of social practices back to the work of Wittgenstein and Heidegger, but the concept is usually associated with scholars such as Bourdieu and Giddens who take practices as a central starting point for understanding social systems. Giddens' theory of structuration (Giddens, 1984) introduces social practices as mediating between actors and structure and places them centre stage: 'The basic domain of study of the social sciences, according to the theory of structuration, is neither the experience of the individual actor, nor the existence of any form of societal totality, but social practices ordered across space and time' (Giddens, 1984: 2). The performance of practices is seen by Giddens as the way that social structures endure or are changed. Continuing to perform an existing practice reinforces or restructures it, whereas changes to the performance by agents will change the practice. If enough changed performances occur, the social structure is changed. Social practices refer to everyday practices and the way these are typically and habitually performed in (much of) a society. Such practices – going to work, cooking, showering – are meaningful to people as parts of their everyday life activities. Practices are said to be social because they are similar for different individuals at different points of time and locations (Reckwitz, 2002). Røpke (2009) argues that the set of elements incorporated in a social practice forms a relatively enduring, self-stabilising pattern. Practices are said to cohere in that they represent a durable collection of elements that are routinely used in a particular way. A social practice is reproduced by individuals and new individuals are recruited to the practice (see Røpke, 2009) and so it captures individuals in a specific behaviour which adds to the reproduction of this practice across space and time.

The concept of social practice is best summed up in this extended quotation from Reckwitz:

> A 'practice' (Praktik) is a routinized type of behavior which consists of several elements, interconnected to one another: forms of bodily activities, forms of mental activities, 'things' and their use, a background knowledge in the form of understanding, know-how, states of emotion and motivational knowledge. A practice – a way of cooking, of consuming, of working, of investigating, of taking care of oneself or of others, etc. – forms so to speak a 'block' whose existence necessarily depends on the existence and specific interconnectedness of these elements, and which cannot be reduced to any one of these single elements. Likewise, a practice represents a pattern which can be filled out by a multitude of single and often unique actions reproducing the practice (a certain way of consuming goods can be filled out by plenty of actual acts of consumption). The single individual – as a bodily and mental agent – then acts as the 'carrier' (Träger) of a practice – and, in fact, of many different practices which need not be coordinated with one another. Thus, she or he is not only a carrier of patterns of

bodily behaviour, but also of certain routinized ways of understanding, knowing how and desiring. These conventionalized 'mental' activities of understanding, knowing how and desiring are necessary elements and qualities of a practice in which the single individual participates, not qualities of the individual. Moreover, the practice as a 'nexus of doings and sayings' (Schatzki) is not only understandable to the agent or the agents who carry it out, it is likewise understandable to potential observers (at least within the same culture). A practice is thus a routinized way in which bodies are moved, objects are handled, subjects are treated, things are described and the world is understood. (Reckwitz, 2002: 49–50)

As was emphasised at the beginning of the chapter, Nicolini (2012) argues that there is not one practices approach, but a number of approaches that have differences and similarities. Nevertheless, it is possible to identify a core set of assumptions and concepts that underlie the general approach and are important to our aims here. Nicolini identifies five core features of the practices approach that would be accepted by most authors in the tradition:

1. The focus on activity, performance and work in the creation and perpetuation of all aspects of social life.
2. The importance of the body and material things in all social affairs.
3. There is a space for individual agency and for initiative, creativity and individual performance.
4. Knowledge is a form of mastery of a particular activity that involves learning and discourse is seen as a way of acting in the world and not just conveying meaning and needs to be considered together with other forms of social and material activity.
5. Power and conflict are constitutive elements of social reality and so practices produce and reproduce differences and inequalities.

A number of aspects of this overall picture are discussed in more detail and the similarities and differences between different authors drawn out.

The meaning of routine

The definitions of social practices outlined in the previous section have included routinisation as an essential element in the performance and identification of a social practice. Schatzki (2019) takes issue with this, arguing that this formulation overplays the stability and continuity of social practices that undermines the emphasis in the concept of structuration on social change. Therefore, Schatzki argues that practices are open-ended and may change with successive performances and this is how social change takes place. His definition is 'practices are open-ended, spatial temporal sets of organized doings and sayings' (Schatzki, 2019: 28). The difference between the two formulations of routine and open-ended can be overemphasised because it seems clear from the literature that there is an acceptance that practices are often performed as routines, such as in the routines of everyday life at home, however, practices are also open-ended in that they may change after performances as the context or elements of the practice change. Change may be intentional or reactive to a change in one or more of the elements. Also, it is important to recognise the differences in the performance of practices. Individuals may have their own unique method of performance, although it may have many similarities with the performances of others that justify its recognition as a common practice. The precise extent of variation that can be accepted may vary according to the empirical context.

Shove et al (2012) recognise that many descriptions of practices represent them as relatively homogeneous entities although they are performed by individuals. Any analysis has the difficult task of generalising from the practices of individuals to more general patterns. Therefore, they argue for a recognition of diversity within practices. Not everyone performs them in the same way. There may be some differences by location, characteristics of the people concerned and so on. Hui makes the distinction between practice as performance and practice as entity. Practice as performance takes place at a particular space and time when understandings, materials, practitioners and activities come together and may not be completely replicable in different situations, times and places. 'Many such performances, undertaken by multiple practitioners in diverse places and times, can be conceptually brought together in considering a practice-as-entity' (Hui, 2017: 55). But the issue then to be confronted is when differences are sufficient to justify the recognition of different practices. This is a very difficult issue that can only be tackled in each particular case and analysts may vary in their interpretations of this. Therefore, there needs to be a recognition of the limits to generalisation that can be made and a realisation that common practices may differ because of a number of variables.

Elements of a practice

The first formulations of social practices focused on social elements such as the behaviours of the actors or agents and their understanding or acceptance of what is involved in performing the practice. However, more recently, and to some degree in response to new materialism, there has been an inclusion of material elements as well (Schatzki et al, 2001; Reckwitz, 2002; Shove et al, 2012). Shove et al (2012: 9) state: 'We take seriously Latour's statement that artefacts are not reflecting (society), as if the reflected society existed somewhere else and were made of some other stuff. They are in large part the stuff out of which socialness is made.'

Activities are routinely performed through the integration of different types of elements, such as bodily and mental activities, material artefacts, knowledge, emotions, skills, and so on. The precise components of a practice identified differ between different authors. Shove et al (2012) define three broad categories of elements of practices; namely, materials, meaning and competence. In empirical studies, these components encompass various more specific elements that are linked within but also across these components to form a 'block' of interconnected elements – the practice. The components are described here and illustrated with the example of bathing:

- *Material* covers all physical aspects of the performance of a practice, including the human body. It is a sequence of bodily activities involving the use of material artefacts. For example, one may take a shower or a bath. Bathing may take place in the morning or the evening, every day or once a week. It may involve materials such as shampoos, soaps and towels, and take place in rooms within the house designed for the specific purpose. Material then covers all activities involved such as purchasing the materials, designing and decorating the bathing room as well as the physical activities of bathing itself.
- *Meaning* refers to the issues which are considered to be relevant with respect to that material, that is, understandings, beliefs and emotions. Issues of relevance associated with bathing are, for example, social norms around cleanliness and privacy, the price, and environmental effect of the energy consumed to heat the water and so on. Bathing may also be associated with ideas of comfort and leisure and the enjoyment of private 'me time'.
- *Competence* refers to skills and knowledge which are required to perform the practice. Examples are knowledge of hot water heating systems as well as ability to pay for them, ability to access baths or showers because of bodily capabilities, and the ability to make the appropriate time available.

These categories are not necessarily mutually exclusive. Schatzki (2019) draws attention to what he terms 'hybrid entities' that can consist of a complex mix of social and material elements. For example, many material elements have a meaning that is socially constructed in addition to their material constitution. Changes in meaning can induce action just as can changes in the material basis. Also, even abstract elements such as thought or discourse have a material basis, whether this is in brain patterns or in the written word on paper or in digital form, and take their form from the performance of practices.

There are disagreements between different authors on the extent of the agency of material objects. For example, Shove et al (2012: 9–10) take issue with Latour's observation that artefacts have the capacity 'to construct, literally and not metaphorically social order'. Nevertheless, they do believe that 'agencies and competences are distributed between things and people, and that social relations are "congealed" in the hardware of daily life'. Schatzki (2019) argues that only humans can undertake practices as they alone can exercise intelligibility and intentionality and operate within a social order. Therefore, while recognising the agency of materials, he suggests that human and material agency need to be kept distinct for analytical purposes. Nicolini (2012: 171) suggests that the common idea is that 'an examination of the world cannot avoid taking into consideration the central role of artefacts and the entanglement between human and non-human performativity'. Also, the practice approach recognises that 'the nature and identity of objects cannot be apprehended independently of the practice in which they are involved – just as we cannot make sense of our practices without taking into account the materials that enter it'. These differences in the place of material and animal elements in practices will be discussed further later in the chapter. However, despite the disagreements, there is universal acceptance of the importance of the more-than-human elements in practices.

Practices often involve routinised bodily activities and movements and so a practice is the product of training and learning to use the body in a certain way. A practice can be understood as the regular, skillful 'performance' of (human) bodies as well as a set of mental activities. Polanyi (1962) uses the concept of 'tacit knowledge' as a way of linking the different forms of personal awareness and knowledge needed to perform a practice with the body in the presence of the material elements. We learn to swing a hammer in a particular way to effectively drive in a nail or learn how to ride a bike through bodily and mental practice rather than from written or verbal instructions (Nicolini, 2012).

Performance of a practice also involves the use of particular things or materials in a certain way that requires specific forms of knowledge or understanding that may be influenced by discursive practices that embrace different forms in which the world is meaningfully constructed in language or in other sign-systems. Nicolini (2012: 5–6) sees discourses as practices as they are not just ways of representing the world but also ways to intervene and act on it. Discursive practices are seen as carrying 'meaning and intentionality onto the scene of action and give actors ways of influencing each other and the situation'. Therefore, discourse in practice theory is seen as one element among many and so should be considered alongside other forms of social and material activity. Critical discourse analysis is seen by Nicolini (2012) as an important technique for studying discourses alongside the social and material conditions that generate them. Schatzki (2017) sees practice theories as adding to existing concepts of discourse by linking them to other forms of action. He argues that:

[S]ayings can be actions of countless sorts, for example, asserting, denying, explaining, asking, complaining, describing, insulting, bothering, ordering, remonstrating, begging, celebrating and so forth. Emphasising multiplicity makes clear that what people are typically about in speaking is, not speaking as such, but performing an action to which the use of language is useful or crucial. (Schatzki, 2017: 132)

He sees discourse as a fundamental component of practice theories, but draws a distinction between theories that see discourse as one and the same as other forms of action and those that see them as linked but different forms. Schatzki (2017: 129) argues that the distinction between these forms of action 'facilitates a more nuanced understanding of what action accomplishes, for example, the varied differences and contributions that doings and sayings make to social existence'. Schatzki sees discourses as being strongly linked to non-discursive behaviours and uses the concept of discourse apparatus to link them in a particular set of ways of talking and thinking:

The environmental discourse coalition, for example, coalesces around such concepts as sustainability, clean energy, saving the Earth, conservation and concern for the future, which it uses in particular ways in speech and writing. The discourse involved can thus be understood as a set of concepts together with their spoken and written (and thought) use in certain constellations of practices and arrangements. (Schatzki, 2017: 137)

It is interesting to note that animals are rarely mentioned as elements in practices. For example, one common routinised practice may be 'walking the dog', in which the dog would be an important element of the practice and its needs, wants and physical attributes and limitations would be one factor in the definition and performance of the practice. It is unclear whether animals are considered in the same category as materials or have different attributes and agency. However, Schatzki (2019) includes four elements in his categorisation of elements of practices including humans, artefacts, organisms and phenomena of nature. He draws attention to the important role of animals in many practices, particularly pets and working animals that are drawn into the personal and social lives. Although he recognises the difficulty in distinguishing between the four elements in some practical situations, he explicitly recognises the specific differences between animals and the other elements: 'they differ from, say artifacts. They move about on their own and do things, and they lead lives that exhibit some, sometimes little and sometimes more than expected, of the complexity, diversity, and psychology of human lives' (Schatzki, 2019: 39).

Schatzki (2019) also draws attention to the role of hybrid elements such as super robots that are materials that may have artificial intelligence that mimics some of the abilities of animals or humans. This general topic is an interesting and important one that we will return to later in the chapter.

The agent

Practices are performed by individuals or agents who are seen as the 'carriers of practices' who do not freely choose between practices based on utility or similar individualistic concepts but are 'recruited' to practices according to their background and history (Reckwitz, 2002). They are neither autonomous nor the judgemental dopes who conform to norms: They understand the world and themselves, and use know-how and motivational knowledge, according to the particular practice. Individuals are seen as the integrators of the elements involved in the performance of the practice and need the appropriate competence to do this. For example, a person may not be able to operate an energy saving heating system or a washing machine because of a lack of understanding, ability to read the instructions and so on. The specific competencies required may vary according to the practice, although there may be some that are general to many practices. Examples may be the ability to read and understand, a physical ability or disability, or a lack of resources, especially financial. It is useless to be able to operate a heating system if a person cannot afford to pay for the electricity. This raises a number of points that will be considered in the following sections, but it is worth drawing attention to the competence issue as it is key to the discussion over whether animals can have practices that will be considered in more detail later.

Also, it is important to recognise that competence may vary between individuals. There is a difference of emphasis among writers in the social practices tradition between a focus on the practice and on the agent and the individual elements that mirrors to an extent the debate within new materialism that was discussed in the previous chapter. Giddens argues that social practices rather than individuals are the basic domain of the social sciences. Shove et al (2012) argue against approaches to public policy that focus on individual behaviour rather than on the practice. But any analysis of a social practice has to focus on the competence of the agent, some part of which will depend on the attitudes, abilities and perceptions of the individual, whether these are deemed to be socially determined or the result of individual physical or mental differences. It is accepted in the social practices tradition that change occurs through individuals varying or altering the performance of a practice (as well as through other factors such as a change in material elements through technology change and so on) and so there is a recognition of the importance of individual agency. So, the position taken here is to adopt the importance of the practice, but to also ascribe agency to the individual agent (as well as to material and other elements involved in the practice). Agents are not just carriers of practices or passive dupes but have individual competencies and characteristics that influence the performance of practices. Therefore, the contention here is that any analysis of a practice needs to include an analysis of the individual agent and of the agency of the individual elements of the practice. For material elements it is necessary to understand their physical attributes because these are important in defining the 'action space' that is possible. Any change in physical attributes may lead to a change in other elements of the practice (such as the expectations and understandings of agents) and in the relationships between the elements.

It is important to note the different causes of change in practices. Schatzki (2019) argues that few changes are intentionally brought about by the performers of a practice. Some may be the product of unintentional change in performance, but others may be reactions to changes in the material or other elements in a practice. Therefore, events and processes may impact on behaviour within a practice. For example, materials have agency because they can induce action in other elements and to the practice as a whole. The impact of material change is mediated through changes in practices that, in turn, have an impact on other elements. Animals may change their behaviour as a reaction to changes in human behaviour as well as because of change in the material world as it impacts on them, such as drought leading to changes in the pattern of plant growth that may result in a change in grazing or migration practices.

Practices are linked

Shove et al (2012) draw attention to the relationships between different practices. A number of practices may use the same elements. In other words, some of the same elements may be reconfigured to constitute a different practice. A number of practices may be linked. For example, in daily life a person may perform a number of routine tasks such as bathing, or washing clothes, or house cleaning, that may use many of the same elements such as hot water and the technology involved in generating this. Practices may be complementary in that they reinforce each other, or they may be competitive in terms of the time of the agent or their resources. The agent may only be able to pay for a limited amount of hot water or may be limited in time to perform domestic activities because of work or caring duties. Schatzki (2019) uses the concept of 'bundles' of practices where the linkages are significant and other authors have used the concept of 'constellations' (Hui et al, 2017). Language, sayings and texts can link together many bundles or constellations of practices by constituting what Shove et al (2012) have termed 'connective tissue'. The interlinking of social practices can make the identification of an individual practice difficult and this is a topic we return to in the next chapter.

As well as being linked, practices may be co-located in the same place. Shove et al (2012) note that some buildings can be the location and focal point of many practices. Schatzki (2019) argues that practices are anchored in a place. One of the most important places is the dwelling or house as it will be the location of many of the practices of daily living. Therefore, what we have termed here inhabitation practices can be central to the lives and lifestyles of many people. However, the absence of a suitable dwelling (as in someone rough sleeping) may make the performance of these practices difficult or impossible, which may have important consequences for the survival and comfort of those involved.

Practices are also linked because of their performance in time. Time is a necessary component of a practice as it is needed for performance. Agents may differ in the use of time for a performance or in their ability to make time available for a performance. Also, the performance of one individual practice follows and is linked to many other practices undertaken both before and after it. Blue (2019) applies the concept of rhythmanalysis to practices, arguing that practices are rhythms that ripple through other practices and elements.

Some practices are more important than others

Some practices may be performed more often than others. Also, practices may vary in their importance to the person performing them. For example, the practice of meal preparation and consumption may be important to health and survival whereas others, such as television viewing, may be seen as less important. Therefore, for these reasons, some practices may be considered to be dominant ones. As Shove et al (2012) note, lives may revolve around a handful of dominant projects, many of which may be concerned with inhabitation.

Practices carry different status rankings

Just as some practices are more important that others, the performance of some have a higher social status. The status may reflect exclusivity or dominant concepts of taste (Bourdieu, 1984). As Shove et al (2012: 54) note: 'By participating in some practices and not others, individuals locate themselves within society and in so doing simultaneously reproduce specific schemes and structures of meaning and order. In Bourdieu's terms, all cultural practices are "automatically classified and classifying, rank ordered and rank ordering" (Bourdieu 1984 p.223).' Related to this is the importance of financial and other resources to the competence to perform a practice. These points are important because they link the concept of social practices to the discussion of inequality. Disadvantage can be conceived as the lack of competence to perform particular important practices whether because of a lack of material resources or any form of competence, whether because of physical ability or lack of access and so on. Within this framework, the commonly used concept of social exclusion can be conceived of as the inability to perform social practices that are considered to constitute the minimum for effective participation in a society.

Social class and inequalities of power are reinforced through the reproduction of dominant practices that are:

> [E]nacted at many levels at once, being reproduced through the daily paths and the life paths of individuals and through the parallel reproduction of institutions, including those of work and family life … the emergence, persistence and disappearances of practices (guided and structured by dominant projects) generates highly uneven landscapes of opportunity, and vastly unequal patterns of access. (Shove et al, 2012: 135)

Power and practices

The concept of relational power is at the heart of the practices approach (Watson, 2017). Power resides in the capacity to act through the relationships involved in a practice. This conception of power includes the capacity for action, which includes the influence on other elements (people, animals and materials) through performance of the practice. Because of their different competencies people may vary in their ability to perform the practices and exert power. Practices may lead to different outcomes in terms of the change that results from them as some practices are more important than others in this regard. Also, access to the practices may vary and be restricted in some way. As a consequence, some people may have the ability to perform many and important practices that may be denied to others.

In addition, some practices may form the context for others. The importance of a practice may be gauged by the influence it has on the performance of other practices by setting the norms or rules by which other practices are performed. One example of this in the field of inhabitation is the impact of the performance of professional practices that may influence the shape of the physical infrastructure of the house as well as regulations that may encourage or prohibit the way that some practices are performed. The practices of manufacturers and sellers of house materials such as soaps or washing machines may provide an important material and social context for the performance of inhabitation practices such as washing clothes. Their practices may have an influence on the regularity of washing, the temperature of the water and so on that may have important impacts on domestic energy use. Therefore, the practices approach recognises the importance of the relations of power both within and between practices and provides a framework for the analysis of inequality in its many guises. It provides a way of unpicking the relationships that structure the way that housing is produced and consumed and the interests that underpin them.

Production and consumption practices

Much of the discussion of social practices uses the examples of consumption practices in everyday life. This has direct relevance for our focus here on the inhabitation practices of daily living within houses and their environs. However, it is important to recognise other practices such as those involved in the production of houses. Shove et al (2012) illustrate this with a discussion of the social practices around the production of concrete and the competences and changes of technology involved. Also, they draw attention to communities of practice that can be based around socialisation into particular careers. Examples in inhabitation practices would be the community of architects, surveyors, planners and builders and so on. Recruits into these occupations are socialised into ways of operating and thinking and to existing institutions and the practices they support and progression in their individual career may be dependent on their absorption and acceptance of these ways. Nevertheless, as Schatzki (2019: 35) points out, there may be substantial differences in the way that individuals perform these professional practices and so 'practices accommodate variation among their participants and in how these individuals carry them on'.

Shove (2017: 155) argues that the concept of practices 'provides a means of connecting otherwise separate realms of producing, manufacturing, making and doing'. This discussion illustrates the possibility and usefulness of the application of the practices framework to production processes as well as consumption ones and both sets are incorporated in our conception of inhabitation practices.

Practices and public policies

Shove et al (2012) argue that the concept of social practices is important as a basis for public policy because of its encapsulation of interconnections and the structural and agency aspects of any issue. Policy prescriptions that focus on change at the individual level, that is, focus on the need to change individual behaviour, neglect the important structural and material elements that influence this. Also, a sole focus on cultural or technical issues may neglect the connections with individual behaviour. An example may be energy saving in the home. The installation of low energy technology may not result in change if the cultural understandings of a warm home counteract this or if no attention is given to the competencies of individuals in coping with the technology. A practices framework allows all of these issues and their interconnections to be considered and a public policy approach adopted that takes them all into account. Analysis of practices enables the relationships and interests that underpin production and consumption of houses to be identified and appropriate points of intervention identified that may enable change to take place.

Practices and assemblages

We shall adopt the term practices and omit the social element in the following discussion as it is evident that the concept is wider than this term would imply. The discussion in this chapter shows that the concept of practices is well suited to a study of inhabitation because of its inclusion of animal and material as well as human elements. Therefore, from henceforth in the book we will link the concept of practices to the concept of inhabitation to form the concept of inhabitation practices. However, the application to the field of inhabitation poses some issues that have to be overcome if it is to be successfully applied and it is to these that we now turn.

There are a number of shared features between the concept of inhabitation practices and the new materialist emphasis on networks and assemblages discussed in the previous chapter and a consideration of these will help in the aim of forging a useful concept in the study of inhabitation.

- Initial depictions of the practices framework did emphasise the social, but more recent work, as illustrated in this chapter, has included a wide range of material, human and animal elements, making it compatible with the new materialist approach.
- New materialism and practices ascribe a unity to the assemblage, network or practice. In other words, it has a coherence and, therefore, needs to be viewed primarily as a whole. The primary focus is then on the interaction of the elements rather than a sole focus on the individual parts. However, within the approaches there are differences between the emphasis of different authors on the analysis of the whole and the constituent parts. Nevertheless, there are similarities in some recent work in both that places a dual focus on individual actants or agents and the whole. Therefore, a twin analytical emphasis on the individual elements and their interactions can be included in both approaches.

It was argued in the previous chapter that there are a number of different grand theories advocated or implicit in the new materialist approaches of different authors. The 'flat' ontology of some versions of new materialism, such as that of Latour, contrast with other versions of new materialism, such as the link with structural forces (as shown in the work of DeLanda) that tend to downgrade the importance of the agency of individuals and networks and see them as secondary to societal forces. The concept of practices grew out of the social theories of writers such as Bourdieu and Giddens. Concepts such as structuration link individual practices with grand, or what some have described as 'meta', theories of society as a whole. However, structuration could be included in a new materialist approach which tends to be a blank canvas on which different social theories can be painted according to the preferences of the individual researcher. However, in the practices approach the structure/agency interaction is integral to the concept and this enables the practices approach to deal effectively with questions of social change (Schatzki, 2019). The new materialist approaches that are not linked with wider social theories can encounter the problems identified with systems approaches of lacking a coherent theory of change, as we shall see in the following chapter.

Issues in the practices approach

Despite the attractions of the practices approach for the aims of this book, there are a number of issues that need to be explored if it is to be successfully applied to the field of inhabitation. Although the concept of practices has been around for some time, recent use has focused around consumption behaviour. For example, when applied to the field of inhabitation the focus has been on consumer practices of households in relation to energy saving technologies and their impact on climate change. This is a valuable approach, but consumer behaviour does not necessarily have to be the sole focus. It is perfectly possible to think in the abstract of the inhabitation practices around the production of housing as well as its consumption. For example, analysis of the inhabitation practice of new housing development would focus on the different human actors involved, the material elements and the animal impacts as well as the interactions between them that result in a particular material outcome in terms of the built form of the house. Even a focus on consumption practices inevitably leads into a study of production processes because the physical structure is a crucial element in the consumption possibilities. The discourses that are part of the production practice and that are made visible through the built form as well as in marketing materials may influence the way that occupants view the house and its use. Therefore, the concept of practices necessarily involves a wider scope than the recent focus on consumption practices would seem to imply and can encapsulate all the elements of housing and inhabitation.

An important question for inhabitation practices is the nature of the agent who performs the practice. As a first step in trying to deal with this important question it is necessary to examine the bases of the practices approach. The most influential author in the approach has been Giddens, who linked it to his theory of structuration. This approach was based on the process in which human agency was linked to social structures through processes of restructuration. In other words, social structures were reinforced or changed through the enactment of practices by individuals. Giddens was at pains to emphasise the importance of human agency in this process but some subsequent applications of the practices approach have downplayed agency and viewed humans as empty vessels of social structures. This opposition can be overcome by recognising, following Braidotti (2019), that humans are 'embodied and embedded'. Action is not just the result of conscious rationality, but the whole scope of bodily feelings, emotions and bodily functions. Also, following Ingold (2000), actors are embedded within a set of relationships and accepted practices that inform their actions. Therefore, an approach needs to be taken that focuses on the perceptions, attitudes and agency of the individuals involved in inhabitation practices and the relationships and structures that encircle them.

A key question is whether this approach can be applied to non-human actors or actants. Maller (2018: 81) argues that 'theories of practice, in the main assume that only people carry practices. From their origins to recent more post-humanist formulations, they rely on the premise of a human practitioner'. Plumwood (2009) identifies a human/nature dualism that is a western-based cultural formation going back thousands of years that sees the mind and consciousness as essentially human and a radically separate order of being from non-human forms which are relegated to 'mere matter', emptied of agency, spirit and intelligence. This reinforces the treatment of non-humans as slaves or mere tools; resources for the use of humans. However, as we shall see in the next few chapters, the agency of materials, animals and other organisms has been the focus of recent attention in practice theory partly because of new materialism. Morley (2017) asks whether machines that share or take over the same tasks as human practitioners can be said to perform a practice? At first glance the focus on the agency of all material and biological organisms may seem a strange proposition because, for example, a tree may seem to be very different from a human. However, the extent of agency among biological wholes may be quite extensive. In other words, the degree of action among plants and animals may be sufficient to warrant attention in any study.

The agency of a material in any context may be generated from other agents that influence the form and the 'possibility space' or agency of a material by their labelling practices. In other words, when studying the tree, it may be important to also study the meaning the tree has for humans because this may impact on the functioning of the tree. Kirksey argues that:

Microbes, and other living beings, clearly interact with our classification practices. Chytrids are certainly torqued as taxonomic scientists care for them by isolating distinct strains, culture them on sterile media, and store collections in refrigerators. Malevolent microbes certainly also respond to human practices of classification and attempts to combat them. Looping effects emerge when microbes mutate, in response to deadly antibiotics, resulting in the proliferation of new kinds of organisms as well as novel scientific and medical practices (cf. Hacking 1999: 105). (Kirksey, 2015: 764)

But it should be recognised that non-human beings may also have meaning and agency. 'The world beyond the human is not a meaningless one made meaningful by humans.' Ecological communities involve other beings with 'relations, strivings, purposes, telos, intentions, functions, and significance' (Kohn, 2013: 72). The world does not consist solely of human meaning, rather there is a multiplicity of worlds and meaning. Wilber (2000) uses the example of a quark to show the importance of the agency of biological organisms, arguing that they do not respond to all stimuli, only to those that have meaning to them, that is, those that affect them. Another example may be the reaction of a deer to a human, which may differ when there is previous experience of hunting. Also, there are some arguments that plants such as trees do communicate with others through their roots (Bridle, 2022). Bennett (2010) argues for a 'vital materialism' that seeks to counter the privileging of a specifically *human* agency or politics by emphasising the agentic contributions of non-human forces in shaping the world. Bennett's effort is to try to comprehend materiality as both in relation to and independent of human life, that is, materiality as a process that sometimes encounters and sometimes exceeds the confines of human life and comprehension. Bennett (2010: 20) theorises materiality within assemblages not as a stable and isolated set of objects, but as a *process* of changing relations between humans and non-humans within assemblages, that is, 'as much force as entity, as much energy as matter, as much intensity as extension'. Part of this vital materialism is to examine the shared experiences of people and materials, 'to take a step towards a more ecological sensibility' (Bennett, 2010: 10). As Bridle (2022: 11–12) notes, when this approach is taken: 'From bonobos shaping complex tools, jackdaws training us to forage for them, bees debating the direction of their swarms, or trees that talk to and nourish one another – or something far greater and more ineffable than these parlour tricks – the non-human world seems suddenly alive with intelligence and agency.'

Ingold (2000) argues against the often-made distinction between humans and animals that can often be seen as a culture/nature divide. In this view, animals are propelled by their 'nature' as in their evolutionary state and have no individual agency. On the other hand, people are propelled by their culture, which is a pre-given and is the lens through which they perceive their environment. Ingold challenges this by means of the ecological psychology of Gibson (1979) and his view of perception. According to Gibson, humans do not perceive their environment through a predetermined cultural filter, but rather see it directly in terms of its affordances to them. This ability to see the use of objects is gained through learning based on an active engagement with the environment through performance in practices. Learning is guided through previous activities that are embodied in established practices or in structures such as buildings and so on. The skills or competence in how to perform in practices is guided by others who have previously performed in them or by structures. Gibson (1979) uses the concept of 'affordance' to understand the interaction of both humans and animals with their environment. He employs the term 'habitat' for the space in which the animal lives and the term 'niche' for the set of affordances that the animal uses. The habitat allows many affordances and an animal fits a niche when there is provision of the right set of affordances for that animal. Like humans, animals act in relation to things according to the significance they hold for them within the setting. The habitat is perceived through the meaning derived through the actions of the animal. Ball (2022) examines the nature of mind for humans and animals and cautions against the often pursued search for elements of the human mind or consciousness. He argues that an animal (just like a human) has its own *Umwelt* that 'reflects what "stands out" for it in the environment: what it notices and what it does not, according to its own set of needs, concerns and capabilities' (Ball, 2022: 169). The mind of an animal has to be seen in this context and thus hierarchies based on human attributes are misleading. The appropriate question to ask is not how a human would act in the specific situation faced by a bat, but, instead, what is it like to be a bat?

Ingold also argues that the process of achieving meaning through action in a particular niche or *Umwelt* is similar for humans and animals. He gives the example of beavers who learn how to build a lodge on the basis of watching their family build them and viewing past examples in their surroundings rather than through their innate evolved instincts. Therefore, he argues that practices are as applicable to animals as humans as both can be classified as 'beings' that have a similar mix of evolved material constitution and skills learned through practices. 'All organisms, including human ones, are not things but beings. As beings, persons are organisms, and being organisms, they – or rather we – are not impartial observers of nature but participate from within in the continuum of organic life' (Ingold, 2000: 90).

Bridle (2022) draws attention to the often-held idea that human intelligence is unique, and uniquely significant in the world. In contrast, he argues that intelligence is an active process and not just a mental capacity. It does not reside inside the head but in the active relationship between elements. 'Intelligence is not something which exists, but something one does; it is active, interpersonal and generative, and it manifests when we think and act' (Bridle, 2022: 51). He shows examples where plants and animals show intelligence. Plants 'hear' caterpillars. Trees communicate. 'I began to realize that the forest was filled with a constant hum of unseen signs and unheard chatter. Decisions were being made, agreements reached, bargains made and broken. The trees were speaking to each other' (Bridle, 2022: 61). He argues that 'plants are more than the sum of a set of pre-programmed actions and reactions. They learn, remember and change their behaviour in response to the world' (Bridle, 2022: 71).

Agency does not have to have an intentional element but may also be reactive. Just as humans can exercise agency by changing their performance in a practice in reaction to changes in material elements, so too may animals. They do not necessarily have to have the same range and depth of competences or consciousness to perform a practice. Animals also have social structures, although the extent and sophistication of these may vary significantly between species. The basis of these is probably a mix between genetic factors and learned knowledge and skills as it is with humans (Ingold, 2000). But this does not eliminate agency. There are many examples of animals changing their behaviour due to changes in their environment. Examples in the UK may be foxes becoming used to an urban environment with the opportunities (and dangers) that offers. Another example of this is the change in location and habitual practices of some seabirds that have learned to live and feed in urban environments such as landfill sites. Animals can adapt and change the practices of which they are an element. Braidotti (2019: 101, original emphasis) argues that 'thinking and knowing are *not* the prerogative of humans alone, but take place in the world, which is defined by the coexistence of multiple organic species and technological artefacts alongside each other'.

Braidotti uses the term posthuman to attempt to overcome the perceived wisdom in the humanities of an opposition between humans and animals, which she regards as being 'too rigid and no longer tenable' (Braidotti, 2019: 10). Gherardi (2017: 38–39) argues that 'the issue is not whether or not materiality matters within practice theory; rather, it is whether materiality merely mediates human activities – as in human-centred theories – or is constitutive of practice, as in post-human practice theories'.

The key to the issue of practice performance is in the definition and distribution of agency. It is important to recognise that agency in a practice is not vested in an individual rational person who performs the practice, but in a complex web of interactions between humans, animals and materials that are elements in the practice. This has been termed a 'distributed agency', which involves an 'interplay of human and nonhuman materialities' (Bennett, 2005: 454). Therefore, in the energy example, Strengers et al

(2016: 766) argue: 'This implies that there is never a single human adult making independent decisions and choices about energy. What may appear as an intentional act is always the outcome of an assemblage, in which agentic capacities are variously, but not necessarily equally, distributed.' Strengers et al use the example of household pets and pests to show the impact that animals can have on household practices:

> Pets and pests cannot speak or make rational decisions like traditional energy consumers, although they might sometimes appear to. Nonetheless, they have ways of expressing and communicating their preferences, needs, likes and dislikes for a range of conditions and resources. They can exercise agency by refusing to eat meals; standing suggestively next to doors, windows and heaters; barking, meowing, hissing, panting, shivering, cooing or chirping; doing things people don't want them to do, such as digging, jumping, scratching, nesting, shitting or eating; and occupying or moving around and between spaces and objects. (Strengers et al, 2016: 770)

The move away from the idea that practices are performed through the intentional actions of humans can lead to a focus on seeing agency as being vested in:

> [T]he elements that co-constitute practice, where meanings are intuitively and socially shared, skills are embodied ways of knowing, and materials are the things drawn on to perform an activity. With this shift away from the conscious human mind, and onto the elements of practice, we can also understand animals as able to perform and participate in practices. (Strengers et al, 2016: 766)

This focus can overcome the problem that, despite the inclusion of material and animal elements in practices, the concept has often been used as a human-centred one in that it is people that perform practices that involve others. In contrast, assemblages have been focused on non-human elements. For example, there could be a study applying the concept to monsoons, with the weather phenomenon being the focus around which the assemblage is assumed to cohere. This raises a number of interesting questions. Is it possible to use the concept of practices in the same way by, for example, studying animal practices? In other words, we may pose what Schatzki argues is a challenging question of whether animals and materials can have practices and whether they are similar to those of humans. Or is the concept of humans or any other actor 'having' or performing practices unhelpful and a more useful focus on the performance of all of the elements in the practice? In other words, humans do not perform practices, rather they perform *in* a practice alongside other elements that also perform in the practice.

The practices emphasis on distributed agency may have an important implication for the way that animals and other organisms are viewed in practices. It would seem to be practicable and useful to apply the practices approach to animals. This would likely provide an insightful contrast and complement to a human-centred approach in a particular circumstance. The research aim would be to identify the different practices that humans and animals perform in and the overlaps or links between them. Taken together they can provide a more holistic picture. This approach could hint at a useful continuing role for the concept of assemblage as it can reinforce a focus on the intersections and differences of practices. We will return to this issue later.

But to take the key question further, can a monsoon have practices? Monsoons do not have conscious agency, but this is not to deny that materials do not have agency that is not in most cases deliberative and conscious as was discussed earlier. But, as argued by Wilber (2000), the dividing line between when it is and is not appropriate to use the concept of practices could be very difficult to draw. He urges researchers to push as much as possible to his lower levels of the hierarchy in order to be as holistic as possible, although decisions will have to be made in particular studies on the basis of practicality and financial availability. Even if a monsoon is deemed not to be a practice of itself, there could be many practices of humans and animals and other materials that are related to monsoons. Monsoons could be seen as a 'connective tissue' (Blue and Spurling, 2017) that binds together many individual practices. In most definitions of assemblage (see Chapter 2) it is accepted that an assemblage consists of practices as well as human, animal and material elements. But as we have argued here, practices also consist of animal and material elements. Therefore, a key question is whether there are important instances of these elements not being captured in practices. In other words, if all the relevant practices were defined and spelled out would there be important elements left over that would be covered in the definition of an assemblage? The difficulties of the agency of materials would suggest that this would not be the case. However, much of the agency of materials is activated in the relationships with humans and animals, and would be explored in the uncovering of their practices. Whether this was the case may vary between different situations and research foci and so may need to be resolved on a case-by-case basis. Schatzki (2019) uses the concept of a 'plenum' to capture the elements that are available to be used in a practice whether or not they actually are used. He argues that this concept is similar to the idea of an assemblage.

A sensible reaction to this issue would be either to use the concept of 'connective tissue' or to try to combine the assemblage and practice approaches. This could involve accepting that, even if the monsoon cannot be the focus of a practice, it can be used as a coordinating device to provide an empirical focus. We argued in Chapter 2 that this is what many assemblage studies tend to do. Most usage of assemblage has been to use the concept as a loose framework and as a reminder to focus on connections and interactions as well as to include human, animal and material elements rather than as a guide to detailed research concepts and methods. A revamped concept of practices, as articulated here, fits well with this general approach by providing a more detailed conceptual framework that can be used in defining a specific research method.

Inhabitation practices and housing pathways

Before continuing to apply the practices approach (together with the concept of assemblages) it is useful to consider its links to the commonly used concept in housing research of housing pathways. One of the foundations of the pathways concept is the structuration approach of Giddens, who saw social practices, ordered in time and space, as the cornerstone of sociological enquiry. Clapham (2005: 27) defines a housing pathway as 'patterns of interaction (practices) concerning house and home, over time and space'. A household's housing pathway is conceived as 'the continually changing set of relationships and interactions that it experiences in its consumption of housing' (Clapham, 2005: 27). As we will discuss in a later section in the chapter, this formulation can easily adopt the wider concept of practice advocated here. Schatzki (2019) argues that practices over time constitute life trajectories and this is very similar to the pathways approach. Housing pathways are constituted by the practices involved.

Another foundation of the pathways approach is social constructionism and this is more problematic. Clapham (2005: 22) says that, in his formulation of the pathways concept, he adopts a weak social constructionism that recognises that the body of an agent and other materials exist, but, because the emphasis is on meaning they are only considered in terms of their social construction. This formulation is unhelpful for the present purpose of studying inhabitation practices for the reasons explored in Chapter 1. However, it is possible to reformulate the approach as it was intended to be holistic in its scope (and this is how it has often been used in practice). The basic step in achieving this is to define practices in the way that has been proposed in this chapter to include animal and material elements as well as to acknowledge the bodily constituents of human functioning. Therefore, the relationships and interactions that the household experiences are with animal and material elements as well as with embodied humans. Within the pathways concept it was conceived that many elements would impact on housing outcomes and the introduction of animal and material elements reinforces this emphasis.

The expanded concept of a housing pathway proposed here would become more explicit if it was to be renamed as an inhabitation pathway and so the inclusion of the wider elements involved in the concept of inhabitation is made clearer. The key differences in this new formulation compared to the initial one are: the acceptance that actants are embodied and have emotions, feelings and physical capacities and constraints as well as socially calculating brains; that practices involve material and animal as well as human elements; and that pathway positions and outcomes include material and animal elements as has been discussed throughout this book. With this reformulation the concept of inhabitation pathways can become a useful research tool that can add extra dimensions to existing research approaches, particularly when it is applied to household consumption practices (it must be remembered that practices as defined here are not only confined to consumption but can also be applied to production and financial processes).

One issue that has been problematised in the pathways approach and in much of housing studies is the question of whether the individual or the household should be taken as the basic unit of analysis. For example, in the study of energy consumption it is common to use the household as the unit of analysis, although the consumer is often viewed as a rational individual. As Strengers et al point out, this assumes:

> [F]irst, that there is one consumer (a Resource Man) who is able to make rational decisions on behalf of the household; second, that the rest of the household agrees with and abides by his or her decisions; third, that people think and make economically rational decisions about their energy consumption; and fourth, that consumers use (energy) data and technology to exert their agency in this process (Strengers, 2013). These assumptions are founded on an understanding of human action that excludes many people, animals and objects, and reproduces a distinctive reality about how energy is consumed and who consumes it. (Strengers et al, 2016: 764)

In this situation it makes sense to use the concept of a household practice because that is the unit within which energy is consumed, although many humans such as teenage household members, babies and pets may have an important role in determining energy consumption.

Operationalising the practices approach

If we are to operationalise the concept of practice, it is important to recognise some issues that may cause problems that may have to be overcome if the approach is to be useful and practicable in studying inhabitation. These issues will form the basis of the discussion in the following chapter of the appropriate research method for the application of the proposed approach.

The first of these issues is the question of how to define a particular practice or assemblage, because there is no widely recognised guidance about how to do this. One approach, favoured by Latour, would be to accept the definitions of key actors. This is an important element in any analysis, but runs the risk of being uncritical of dominant definitions and discourses. Another approach would be to look for practices that are cohesive or show a 'stickiness'. In practice it may be difficult to define or quantify and recognise the limits or boundaries. This may account for the empirical difficulties in some studies in knowing where to draw the line. There may be a trade-off between breadth and depth of analysis. Blue and Spurling (2017) argue that the focus of any analysis should be 'a complex' of practices rather than an individual one and use the concept of 'connective tissue' to refer to the important elements that bind individual practices together and so have a more general impact. The search for a consistent approach to these issues of identification and scope may be unnecessary and limiting. It could be argued that there is substantial value in being open to varying approaches and to adopting a framework that is appropriate to different objectives and situations. Perhaps the need then is to have criteria of rigour in the analysis rather than a fixed method.

The second problematic issue is the balance in any analysis between individual elements and the interactions between them. In both assemblage and practices approaches there is an ongoing tension between a focus on the individual actant and the whole (network, assemblage or practice), and individual authors within each tradition take very different views. As noted in Chapter 2, some authors within the new materialist approach focus on the whole as shown through the interaction between actants rather than on the actants themselves. some readings of the practice approach treat individuals as 'empty dupes' that are defined by the practices and their structural and interactionist elements. Therefore, practices are seen as the 'smallest unit' of social analysis. In contrast, other studies combine a focus on the whole and on the individual actants as it is argued that failure to do so undermines the importance of individual agency that are important to, for example, the structuration approach of Giddens. In this latter approach the precise mix of the individual and the whole is contingent on the precise situation and context and so becomes an empirical issue. Therefore, a research method is required that can be used to analyse both these elements and to be holistic in terms of the quadrants identified by Wilber (2000), which we will discuss in Chapter 4.

The third important issue is how to capture the analysis of individual, very different elements. Analysis of any network, assemblage or practice involves treatment of many different kinds of phenomena including human, animal and material. Wilber (2000) has devised a useful framework for this as we will see in Chapter 4, but the difficulty here is in analysing the different elements that have been the focus of very different approaches in the past. For example, the scientific study of materials using concepts from positivist science does not sit well with the sociological study of people and societies that uses a variety of approaches but rarely uses a positivist scientific framework. The key question is how they can be reconciled when the study is of the interaction of these phenomena. Although Wilber (2000) gives a general framework for this, he gives less guidance on how the different elements inherent in his quadrants are to be brought together and reconciled.

Conclusion

This chapter has focused on the third proposition outlined in Chapter 1 that the concept of practices is the primary focus for the examination of inhabitation. This approach gives the analysis a precision not always apparent in new materialist approaches, which have often been ambiguous and confused about the links with wider social theory and about the specifics of the approach. However, the focus of new materialist approaches on networks and assemblages is a useful one. Therefore, the way forward proposed here is to embed new materialism into the practices approach in order to make the most of the benefits of both. Inhabitation practices sit within, as well as constituting, networks and assemblages but are the primary analytical focus if important issues are to be investigated and public policy to be formulated and evaluated.

The practices approach offers a holistic framework for examining linguistic and material aspects of housing while dealing satisfactorily with questions of agency and structure and providing a practical research framework. A focus on practices can offer the advantages of both the constructionist and materialist approaches by integrating language and material–human interactions within a holistic analysis. At present studies using this framework have focused on areas of housing consumption, but the approach has the potential to be applied more generally and to fulfil the desire of Kemeny for a theoretically aware field of housing studies. However, there are many issues that need to be resolved if the approach is to be usefully applied to the field of inhabitation and this is the focus of Chapter 4.

4

Analysing inhabitation practices

In the previous chapters, the concepts and general approaches involved in the analysis of inhabitation and inhabitation practices were laid out. The aim of this chapter is to provide more detail on the analytical and research processes involved and to highlight some of the issues to be confronted in the choice of methods and evaluation criteria to employ. Therefore, the chapter focuses on the fourth proposition outlined in Chapter 1, to adopt a holistic research method to study inhabitation practices. The key question to be addressed is how should inhabitation practices be studied and evaluated by academics, governments or housing agencies? The answer to this question will depend on the precise aims and context of a particular research study and the issue on which it is focused, however, the aim of the chapter is to outline some of the general issues involved and the choices available.

Inhabitation practices include human, animal and material elements, and it was argued in the previous chapter that a blended approach to empirical research was needed that would examine the relationships and interactions between elements in a practice as well as the agency of the individual actants. But this leaves open the key question of how they can be related together and studied given the very different traditions of enquiry involved in existing research on the human, animal and material elements. This is not a new problem or one unique to housing studies, but an issue that has held back research in general. One reason for the difficulties in the adoption of new materialism is the lack of a holistic approach and a language that can integrate the study of these different phenomena and then to use this to devise an appropriate method of analysing and researching them.

The term *holistic* has been used throughout the book and it is worth spending some time explaining here what is meant by this. Holistic is defined in the Merriam–Webster dictionary as 'relating to or concerned with wholes or with complete systems rather than with the analysis of, treatment of, or dissection into parts'. This conception is based on the idea that the whole is greater than the sum of the parts and contradicts the idea that segmentation or the breaking down of knowledge into dualisms such as humans/nature or mind/body is an appropriate form of knowledge. Perhaps the most well recognised use of the term is in holistic medicine, which aims to include both mind and body. Academic disciplines tend to segment knowledge of the world and confine their attentions to one field with a particular methodology that uncovers only part of the overall picture. A method that aims to be holistic tries to see the parts of any phenomenon in relation to the whole. Therefore, the practice approach can claim to be holistic in its scope and aims. This does not mean that the ideal of total and complete understanding can be attained because of the difficulties of gaining knowledge of complex and changing phenomena and combining different insights. Nevertheless, adoption of the idea does involve acceptance of this as a guiding principle and the aim of being as comprehensive as possible given knowledge and practical constraints. As we shall see in this chapter, most difficulty can occur in attempting to combine different insights into a complete view of a phenomenon. In some instances, the aim to be holistic may be constrained to just seeing something from a number of different angles. Nevertheless, the problems caused by a priori adoption of the dualisms that have been highlighted in the book mean that the aim of holism is a worthwhile one.

The first focus of this chapter is to move towards a holistic analysis using the ideas of the philosopher Ken Wilber to elucidate aspects of the practices framework. He argues that any phenomenon is made up of quadrants that each need to be investigated using appropriate methods and integrated into a holistic analysis. It must be stressed that the ideas of Wilber are not intrinsic to the concept of practices and they are put forward here as one possible way of applying the practices framework and other ways are possible. Nor is his approach an alternative to the practices framework. Rather, it can best be seen as reinforcing some trends in existing practices research.

The discussion will then examine the empirical analysis of inhabitation practices. The first focus will be on the problematic process of identifying an inhabitation practice to study. The chapter continues with a discussion of each of the quadrants of a holon identified by Wilber, examines the choices of research method and evaluation criteria that would be possible and appropriate in each quadrant for the examination of inhabitation practices, and outlines some of the most important issues involved. The vital issue of the integration of data from the different research methods that are used in the analysis of the quadrants is then discussed in the following section in order to provide a holistic analysis. The chapter concludes with a discussion on how inhabitation practices can be evaluated and provide useful information for policymaking by governments and housing organisations.

Towards a holistic analysis

Approaches to the examination of the physical environment tend to be based on the 'scientific method' consisting of positivist, empirical, 'black box' studies. The evaluation of worth is based on input/output studies in which a given stimulus is assessed on the basis of its output. An example would be a medical clinical trial in which the worth of a particular drug or treatment regime is based on a comparison between an experimental group and a placebo group which are matched on a number of criteria. There is no specific focus on what happens in the 'black box' or interior, with the outcome (or success) being judged on an empirical analysis of the impact of the drug (allowing for other confounding variables) on certain measurable symptoms or disease markers, although it is usually considered valuable to have a plausible theory to guide the research. The emphasis in this approach to knowledge is on the observable or surface phenomena that can be observed by a 'neutral' observer and replicated by others in different contexts. As well as the empiricist approach to knowledge, the scientific research paradigm often makes use of a systems analogy as in concepts such as the solar system, the human body or the ecosystem. An implicit assumption of the systems approach is that of self-regulation and harmony. Illness or damage is caused when this self-regulation breaks down. For example, problems are said to occur in the ecosystem when the system is disrupted and ceases to function in a sustainable or acceptable way through, for example, human activity leading to climate change and global warming.

The construction of a unified language for researching the different elements of practices is made difficult because this empiricist and positivist approach is not the usual one taken in the social sciences. There may be some areas (some fields of economics, psychology, and so on) where the approach may be accepted by some, but these fields have not generally been integrated into the rest of social science. For example, behavioural economics has seen the integration of some positivist traditions of economics with aspects of psychology that share a similar philosophy in their research approach and have not been integrated with mainstream sociology or geography that generally are based on different paradigms. In sociology and other social science disciplines, the positivist and functionalist elements of the scientific approach are usually associated with traditions such as structural-functionalism and authors such as Talcott Parsons that are not commonly used or fashionable today. These traditions usually emphasise the relationships and interconnections between elements rather than the individual elements themselves and judge their success by their function or contribution towards the whole. In contrast, approaches in the hermeneutic tradition, such as social constructionism, have focused on the internal world of individuals and societies and can be criticised as neglecting the function of the whole.

New materialist approaches such as assemblage and ANT have many similarities with the systems approach with their emphasis on interconnections and the 'health' or function of the whole. Wilber (2000) includes these as part of what he labels as a new systems science that is evident, for example, in the concept of an ecosystem. He argues that these approaches have their strengths in the focus on wholeness and interconnectedness but they are only partial in that they neglect subjectivity and agency and what Wilber terms 'interiority'. In other words, unlike hermeneutics, they focus on what the universe looks like from the outside rather than how it looks from the inside. Systems theories in general can be criticised in their treatment of system change which tends to emphasise adaptation to the environmental context (or the situation within which it is situated and relates to) of the phenomenon being investigated. Some versions of systems theory assume that systems are self-regulating and stabilising, and are moving automatically towards an equilibrium. For example, the concept of an ecosystem is sometimes associated with the belief that humans have 'interfered' in self-stabilising ecosystems causing dysfunction, and that, if left alone by humans, equilibrium would resume. However, this approach seems to deny human as well as animal and material agency as well as perpetuating the harmful separation of society and nature that was outlined in Chapter 1. Even versions of systems theory such as the concept of the 'eco principle' advocated by Dahl (1996) in which he advocates a symbiosis between human and natural eco systems, still focus on the external collective dimension and ignore interiority. Despite this drawback, Lawrence (2021) proposes the principle as a framework for the design of built environments that are sensitive to 'natural systems'.

Another weakness of system theory is the assumption of a harmonious whole. Wilber (2000: 137) argues that the dominant theme of the Enlightenment was the 'harmony of an interlocking order of being', a systems harmony that was behind most forms of thought. When applied to the human body this seems to make sense. It would be uncomfortable and harmful to the health of the whole for one part of the body to be fighting others. However, when applied to societies or ecosystems, this assumption seems to hide potentially important issues. Alternative conflict-based views of society would see the whole being characterised by warring social classes or other status or lifestyle or cultural divides.

Wilber's argument is that systems theory tends to claim to be holistic and all-encompassing, but in fact it is partial and neglects the key issues involved in the study of interiority. He states that (2000: 87) 'it is not that systems theory is wrong; it is that ironically, it is incredibly partial and lopsided'. So, the problem is how to hold a conversation or even to integrate the human, animal and material elements through the physical and the social sciences that have such different approaches. New materialism claims to have developed an approach that creates an integrated analysis of human and non-human actors. However, there is still a problem in integrating this type of analysis with scientific studies of the material world because of their different assumptions and concepts as well as problems around the integration of the exterior and interior views. Without a common 'language' it becomes difficult to integrate the human world and the rest of Nature, which is the aim here. Do social scientists have to discard their current approaches or is there a way of creating a common language?

Bennett (2010) uses the term *monism* to refer to the idea that everything is made up of the same 'stuff' and one useful application of this approach is provided by Ken Wilber (2000) who builds on the concept first formulated by Arthur Koestler (1967) of the holon. Wilber argues that all matter is made up of 'holons' which are at the same time wholes and parts of a whole (whole/parts). Starting from the 'Web of life', with the whole kosmos, he argues for a holonic or holistic theory of everything. According to this theory, wholes/parts are (obviously) made up of any mixture of material, animal or social matter. He argues that holons are in hierarchies (which he calls levels) with those on lower levels being more basic. A higher level holon can be destroyed without necessarily destroying those in levels below it. However, it cannot be destroyed without also destroying those above it. Generally, the higher the level of the holon the more complex it is. For example, a molecule is a higher level holon than an atom as all molecules could be destroyed but atoms could still exist. In the same way, societies or cultures could be destroyed but people could still exist. Wilber uses the concept of 'levels' or the hierarchy of holons to theorise the relationship between people and the rest of Nature. He differentiates between three related holons that make up the kosmos: the physiosphere (matter); the biosphere (life); and the noosphere (the mind). These are levels of a hierarchy in which each level transcends but includes the lower levels. So, the biosphere includes but transcends the physiosphere as life has a physical basis; but it in turn is transcended and included in the noosphere as the mind has a basis in both. Among other things, this dissipates the often-made schism between people and Nature as humans are part of nature and share all elements of it. Wilber uses the term Nature to include people and animals and materials and this terminology has been followed in this book.

Wilber continues by arguing that all holons have four quadrants according to the different perspectives that can be taken on those holons (abbreviated to AQAL) (see Figure 4.1).

One axis of the AQAL is interior/exterior. An exterior view of a holon is based on observable behaviour and is the perspective that positivist empirical study takes on both individuals and collectives. The interior view is the perspective taken from within the holon, that is the subjective perspective, for example, as done in hermeneutics studies from within collectives and in phenomenological studies from within individuals. It is based on the range of sensations, attitudes, perceptions, use of concepts and symbols and so on of the holon. The second axis is individual/collective holons, for example individual humans or human societies. The upper-left quadrant, which is individual and interior, is labelled intentional as it involves the sensation of the individual holon. The upper right is individual and exterior, which focuses on the observable behaviour of the individual holon. The lower right is collective and exterior labelled the social (system), although it can include systems such as galaxies and ecosystems as well as social organisations

Figure 4.1: Quadrants of a holon

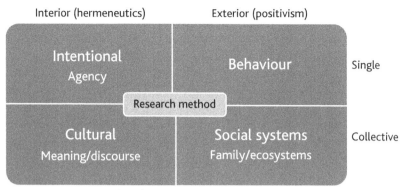

Source: Adapted from Wilber (2000)

such as families, societies and so on. The lower left quadrant is labelled the cultural and is interior and collective. This can involve the study of meaning, symbolism, language and discourse. This involves the shared interior meanings or worldview.

Wilber's key point is that all elements will be present in a holon, although the precise balance may differ, sometimes considerably. He is unequivocal that 'every holon has at least these four dimensions (or four quadrants) of its existence, and thus it can (and should) be studied in its intentional, behavioural, cultural, and social settings. No holon simply exists *in* one of the four quadrants; each holon *has* four quadrants' (Wilber, 2000: 135, original emphasis). As we argued in Chapter 3, the degree of agency among materials, plants and animals may be sufficient to warrant attention in any study and the concept of distributed agency means that all elements need to be considered together. Wilber argues that the importance of the interior grows with the existence of consciousness in a holon, but he leaves the question of how far down you push the existence of consciousness to individual researchers. However, he argues that there should be an awareness of the possibility of its existence and an exploration of ways to explore it in order to avoid issues of anthropomorphism that could occur if observable, surface behaviour was to be used instead. Although any internal state has its equivalent surface reflection as shown in behaviour, there is a need to interpret behaviour and so anthropomorphism could happen with humans interpreting animal behaviour in the light of human characteristics. To act unreasonably by ignoring the meaning elements of behaviour is to be reductionist as Wilber argues systems theories are.

Wilber argues that there should be a unified concept of appropriate science to investigate the four quadrants that moves beyond existing concepts of positivism and scientific rigour based on it. He argues that:

> To say that an inquiry is following the disposition of good science is not to say what the *content* or *actual methodology* of that inquiry will be. It only says that this inquiry engages the world (injunction), which brings forth experiences of the world (data), which are then checked as possible (confirmation). But the actual form of the inquiry – its methods and its content – will vary dramatically from level to level and from quadrant to quadrant. (Wilber, 2000: 78, original emphasis)

Wilber continues by arguing that each of the quadrants should be evaluated by different criteria. The right-hand two quadrants can be studied through the empirical observation of behaviour, which he argues is important, but not the whole picture. The left-hand quadrants necessitate getting into the interior of the holon and so require interpretation and study that focuses on meaning, not just what can be seen. The right-hand quadrants can be evaluated by analysis of 'what does it do?' whereas the left-hand quadrants require assessment of 'what does it mean?'. The top right quadrant can be assessed by the truth of the observation and the bottom right by the accurate description of the functional fit of the holons. How do they function and what do they do? The left-hand quadrants can be assessed by the truthfulness (rather than truth) of individuals and the mesh of intersubjective understanding of the lower left quadrant judged by the subjective values of ideas of justice or rightness. Therefore, any assessment should include not just the truth of objects, or truthfulness of subjects, or the mesh of intersubjective understanding (justice or rightness), but also the functional fit (mesh of interobjective relations 'what does it do'?).

Of course, not all organisms or holons can flourish. A simple example is that one predator may flourish but at the expense of its prey. Therefore, some judgement needs to be taken about the respective value of holons. It is common in the ecological movement to ascribe equal value to all living things, but this seems to ignore the dilemmas involved. Policy makers are used to making these decisions with regard to people as almost every decision/policy has distributional impacts as some people will gain and others will lose. Moral values have been used to decide among competing interests such as values of equality that can be used to aid in these choices. Wilber agrees that all holons have 'intrinsic value' but is critical of the idea of the equality of organisms. He argues (2000: 544–546) that holons differ in their depth, that is, some consist of more holons than others and these are, therefore, more significant to the kosmos as a whole because they incorporate more of other levels. Also, holons vary in their value to other holons that will depend on them. The greater the dependence, the more extrinsic value the holon will have. This argument leads Wilber (2000: 546) to the conclusion that 'it is much better to kill a carrot than a cow'. This position of Wilber is not one that will be universally shared and stems from his belief in an evolutionary perspective that can see a progression from lower to higher organisms and levels of organisation that can seem to be deterministic without specifying the mechanisms that generate this movement. However, it is possible to derive other value statements about the worth of different organisms without jettisoning other aspects of Wilber's analysis. Another version of the value systems involved is present in the conservation and rewilding debate where emphasis is placed on what may be termed 'keystone' or 'functional' species that are said to have a large impact on the ecology of particular spaces and landscapes (Jepson and Blythe, 2020). Much attention has focused on the large predators and herbivores that are said to create the conditions in which other species can flourish and a balanced ecosystem result. In practice, the valuation of the worth of different forms of animal species between those of the conservationists and Wilber may not differ too much with both focusing on more developed forms of life that would be high on Wilber's evolutionary chain.

At first glance the disaggregation of the quadrants would seem to contradict one of the key elements of the practice approach, which is the creation of being through the performance of practices (see Chapter 3). It was argued in the previous chapter that agents are not just carriers of practices or passive dupes but have individual competencies and characteristics that influence the performance of practices. Therefore, it was contended that any analysis of a practice needs to include an analysis of the individual agent and of the agency of the individual elements of the practice. It was recognised, following Braidotti (2019), that humans are 'embodied and embedded'. Action is not just the result of conscious rationality, but the whole scope of bodily feelings, emotions and bodily functions. Also, following Ingold (2000), actors are embedded within a set of relationships and accepted practices that inform their actions. Therefore, an approach needs to be taken that focuses on the perceptions, attitudes and agency of the individuals involved in inhabitation practices and the relationships and structures that encircle them.

An important criticism of Wilber is that, while emphasising the need for a holistic analysis, he places considerable focus on the disaggregation of the holon through study of the quadrants without a corresponding discussion of their integration beyond arguing that all elements should be considered. The first step in resolving this is to emphasise the relationships between the different quadrants rather than to see them as existing independently. In other words, the elements of the holon are just different perspectives on the same phenomenon. The external perspective may view the embodied behaviour of people and animals in practices, but the internal element is what the practice means to them in terms of their embodied feelings and understanding. Both elements are needed in the analysis of practices and need to be combined. Wilber's disaggregation of the elements of the holon is primarily a reminder that all the quadrants are important as they are related together and all are needed for a holistic analysis of practices, whereas many research traditions have produced a partial picture by only focusing on one or two.

One of the keys to understanding the different elements of the whole is the stipulation of different evaluation criteria for the different quadrants. This means that there will not be a single and simple answer to the functioning and outcomes of practices. On the one hand this could be considered a hindrance to policymaking, but on the other hand it may be useful in highlighting the different factors involved and making choices explicit. We will return to this topic in a later section.

The problem of the separation of quadrants is particularly important when applied to the concept of inhabitation practices where the emphasis is both on individual actants and their relationships. This problem can be overcome by focusing on the relationships between holons and the different levels. For example, actants can be seen as holons themselves, but the practice they perform in is also a holon at a higher level. Therefore, any analysis should not be overly focused on one level, but should move between levels to capture the complex interplay involved.

Wilber's contribution to practices

Wilber's framework leaves some issues unresolved, such as how the reconciliation of the different elements in the approach should take place, nor does it give any indication of how different forms of knowledge are to be prioritised in particular situations. Also, the framework does not provide the detailed guidance necessary to relate the overall framework to the study of a specific field such as that of inhabitation attempted here. In addition, there may be some reservations about Wilber's evolutionary perspective. As was noted earlier, it is possible to operationalise the practices framework without adopting an approach based on Wilber, as studies quoted in the next chapters will show. However, his analysis provides a useful way of providing an integrated language in which to situate the study of the interaction between people and the material and animal world, and offers a general way forward that is useful as part of the jigsaw involved in the study of inhabitation. Therefore, it is worthwhile drawing out some of the general points from the overall framework outlined here:

- Wilber's analysis could be construed as being in contradiction to the idea of a discrete social science. It is clear any analysis needs to examine the interaction between the human and other forms of matter as well as seeing the human as embodied and so breaking down the mind/body dualism. This view endorses the approach taken in studies in the new materialist tradition and the practices approach outlined in the previous chapter.

- The analysis of the quadrants of a holon reinforces the concern in some versions of practice theory on the agency of the individual elements of a practice and not just on the whole.
- Wilber's emphasis on the interior and the exterior aspects of a practice and the agents involved is a useful guide for a holistic research focus.
- The analysis of the quadrants places an emphasis on the necessity of the use of different research methods to examine the different elements of a phenomenon. It demands a reconciliation between different traditions of science to examine the exterior and the interior elements of a holon.
- The use of the quadrants also highlights the need for evaluation criteria that reflect all four elements. This implies the use of multiple criteria.

Wilber's analysis highlights the partial nature of much existing thinking on environmental issues. The generally accepted divide between humans and 'nature' was discussed in Chapter 1. A Nature that is devoid of people and their world is often linked with the concept of an ecosystem that is usually investigated through scientific enquiry. In terms of Wilber's quadrants, in this approach knowledge is derived from the lower-right quadrant of collective behaviour and is evaluated on the basis of the function of the whole. However, in addition to the drawbacks of systems theory identified earlier, this type of analysis misses the important elements in the interior quadrants. Therefore, it lacks a useful theory of human and animal behaviour in particular, which is important if change and the role of individual and group agency of humans and animals is to be understood. In the dehumanised and scientific idea of Nature that humans have despoiled or degraded, it is easy to adopt the idea that humans should leave Nature alone for it to heal itself, rather than to accept that human action through change in lifestyles and social practices is necessary to formulate effective proposals for the wellbeing of all elements of Nature. The three elements of materials, animals and humans are linked in Nature and to bring about change, a way is needed of relating these together in a coherent and holistic way.

Towards a research method for inhabitation practices

The practices approach offers insight into the relationships between humans, animals and materials with its focus on the importance of the interconnections. The insights offered by Wilber help to show the drawbacks of some versions of new materialism that bear a resemblance to general systems theories, such as the lack of an interior view of actants and a limited focus on the agency of individual actants. Any study of a practice needs to understand the nature of the elements of which it is composed and so what is needed in the practice approach is a focus on both actants themselves as well as their interactions. Both should consider the interior and exterior view covering all the quadrants identified by Wilber.

The primary focus in the practice approach is on the individual practices and so the analysis will begin with a discussion of their identification. Important questions include the criteria to be used in deciding on the existence of a practice and how it relates to bundles or constellations of practices and the role of connective tissue in relating them together. The discussion then moves on to the analysis of the different elements of a practice and the insights gained from Wilber's analysis are used to guide this.

The general approach proposed here is to focus primarily on the individual practice, but to 'zoom in and out' (Nicolini, 2012) in a three-stage process. Zooming in, as used here, involves the study of the individual elements of the practice in more detail than is sometimes done in assemblage applications. Zooming out involves situating the practice among the bundle of practices, connective tissue and networks that surround it in space and time.

Identifying an inhabitation practice

One of the problems outlined earlier has been the difficulty of identifying and delimiting an inhabitation practice. How do you know when a practice exists? How can you define it? Where do you stop in your analysis? Is it more important to define an inhabitation practice or a bundle of practices or a 'connective tissue' between them in the first instance? Are the concepts of a network or assemblage or practice bundle useful here? The process of identification is important because of the need to find a feasible and useful way of analysing a subset of an almost infinite mesh of relationships and connections. An approach has to be feasible within the practical and resource constraints that any study or organisation faces. Also, the approach has to be useful in that it furthers understanding of the field and offers information that can contribute to government policymaking and to the operational and strategic decision-making processes of private and public housing agencies. An important part of any discussion on the evaluation of the activities of these agencies is the consideration of policies and programmes. Are they most usefully seen as practices, bundles of practices or connective tissue?

The difficulties of finding a way to unravel the complex and interconnected realities of assemblages and networks have led some authors, such as Latour, to propose a focus on the assemblage construction process as a way of identifying assemblages and cutting through the web of interconnections that can embed practices. The justification for this approach is that this is the time that assemblages become more visible and so easier to identify and study. However, this approach has the potential drawback of ignoring the mass of long-standing existing assemblages and practices and so there is a need for a way of identifying them.

There is no one objective or right way to define a practice and it may depend on the particular objectives and resources of individual research projects or analyses. However, there are indicators that can be used to assess whether a particular identification is appropriate, such as the concept of adhesiveness that has been used in the study of assemblages and networks. In other words, assemblages have a coherence and fixity that enables them to 'stick together' and endure over time while resisting destabilising factors. The same standards of coherence and fixity may be applied to inhabitation practices, although these standards are very vague and difficult to apply. How long does a practice have to be fixed? Does the criterion of fixity lead to a lack of recognition of practices that change rapidly, but may be important nevertheless? In a similar vein, how is coherence to be defined? How 'tight' do the actants and their interactions in a practice have to be? Can this be measured in terms of the intensiveness of interaction that may be seen as a function of the number of interactions in a particular time period and the importance attached to them by the actants? One criterion for the choice of inhabitation practice could be that it is recognisable and important to the human participants. However, some practices may not be recognised as such by the participants and their rating of importance may not correspond with the importance of the practice to other humans or to animal or material participants.

The lack of an agreed set of rules for identifying an inhabitation practice means that there is scope for different approaches to the task. This flexibility is a strength in that it allows for insight to be generated by examining a phenomenon from a number of different directions. For example, one definition could focus on practices as defined by human participants and another on those that take animal practices as the focal point. Much of the content may be the same, but the different focus may enrich understanding of the practices under review and their impacts by 'seeing a phenomenon' from different viewpoints.

It is important to recognise that the starting point for an analysis of inhabitation practices does not have to be the practices themselves. In Chapter 2 it was argued that the concept of assemblage could be used as a connecting device to identify the factors (including practices) that are related to a particular phenomenon and we are proposing an approach that makes appropriate use of this concept alongside that of practices. It is important to recall that the concept of an assemblage was considered by many authors to be similar to that of a bundle or constellation of practices (see Chapter 3). Therefore, an assemblage or practice bundle can be used as an integrating concept that enables the identification and study of relevant practices. The starting point for the identification of an inhabitation practice could be an assemblage focused on a particular outcome. For example, the production of a new house may be a good starting point for the identification of one or a number of practices that are relevant to this outcome. Different geographical or other levels may be appropriate depending on the aims of the research study. For example, the focus could be the production of one house, but the analysis could take in the whole process including issues such as finance, land provision, planning and construction. Another approach could be to examine the general processes for new development but to focus on one aspect of it such as the type of construction process employed. In all instances there needs to be a cognisance of the context within which the specific analysis takes place. Insights derived from studies with different starting points may be possible if contextual factors are appropriately considered.

One of the focuses in this book is on the evaluation of policy and so the identification of a policy as the starting point for the study of the social practices involved is an important one. For example, the discourses, animal, human and material elements, and their interactions that are related to a particular policy and make up an inhabitation practice can be studied in this way. The policy could be conceived as being the assemblage around which a variety of social practices are situated or as a connective tissue. An example could be the policy towards street sleeping. There is not one policy here but a web of interconnecting policies which could be taken together or, alternatively, an individual element isolated which could be a recent change in policy. Within the assemblage or bundle there will be numerous inhabitation practices. One may cohere around the daily lives of street sleepers themselves. Another may be the practice of daily life in emergency hostels and shelters. There would be choices to make about the scope of the analysis and the practices on which to focus more specifically depending on the research aims of the particular study.

The same approach may be used to analyse the impact of particular programmes of housing agencies. For example, an agency could examine the impact of a particular housing development by investigating the inhabitation practices involved in its construction and occupation. More examples of the research approach will be given in the following chapters.

Studying the quadrants

The identification of a practice is the key initial step in any analysis. As we have discussed earlier, in some versions of practice or new materialist approaches the interactions involved in the performance of the practice would be the primary, if not only, focus. However, we have argued here for a three-stage approach that analyses the overall practice and its individual elements and actants as this is crucial to understanding actual and potential change in the practice, as well as situating the practice in space and time. Therefore, the analysis should start with identification and analysis of the practice, but should also delve down into the individual elements and out to the context.

In this section the quadrants of a holon identified by Wilber will be used to frame a discussion on the research approach and techniques that are appropriate for the study of inhabitation practices. The discussion will be divided into the individual quadrants for ease of exposition and to illustrate the detailed elements that will make up the whole analysis, but it is important to bear in mind the interrelations between them and the need for their eventual integration. As we have already argued, individual actants are holons, but so is the practice in which they perform and each quadrant at each level needs to be investigated. The following discussion will consider the application of the analysis based on the quadrants to both the social practice and the elements of which it is comprised.

It was stated in Chapter 3 that a practice can involve body, mind, things, knowledge, routines and individual actants. Performance of the practice will involve interaction between the different elements. In a different formulation it is stated that practices involve material, meaning and the competence of individual actants. In another way of seeing this, practices involve feelings, actions and interactions. The research method employed needs to be able to uncover all of these different elements and so needs to be comprehensive, holistic and integrated. The quadrants will be analysed from the point of view of humans, animals and materials as each may need different research methods and techniques.

Interior/individual (upper left) quadrant

The aim in this quadrant is to understand the interior sensations, perceptions, emotions and understandings of the holon. These may cohere into 'ways of seeing the world' and to discourses and stories that enable actants to make sense of the world and their place in it and to understand the nature of appropriate behaviour in different settings. Bourdieu labelled this the habitus and it is integral to the concept of practices that is the basis of the approach proposed here. In this way the individual and collective interior quadrants are linked, as we will discuss later, as well as the links between the interior states and the exterior behaviour.

For studying the interior states of human actants there is a strong tradition of hermeneutic research that can underpin the choice of particular research techniques for each study. The techniques include individual or group interviews as well as techniques designed to enable researchers to understand what is in the individual's conscious and unconscious mind as well as uncover their emotions or feelings. Insights from this tradition may be added to from within the tradition of positivist psychological research on issues such as brain states. Insight on some issues can be gained from integration of these perspectives as well as uncovering the links between this and other quadrants such as behaviour (upper-right quadrant).

It has been argued throughout the book that the agency of animals is important, but the uncovering of thought and emotions is problematic because of the communication difficulties involved. However, Maller (2018) argues for the use of an ethnographic sensibility to research with animals and argues that multispecies ethnographies are also aligned with ideas from the biological sciences that are beginning to re-personalise and enliven research with non-human animals, using techniques such as critical anthropomorphism (Burghardt, 2007), which is used to understand complex animal emotional states and ways of being in the world once thought unique to humans, such as the use of tools and other materials in foraging for and consuming food, and attracting mates. Burghardt (2007: 137) argues that critical anthropomorphism involves the use of a wide range of tools and knowledge from different disciplines: 'We need to use all our scientific and natural history knowledge about a species, including its physiology, ecology, and sensory abilities to develop testable hypotheses, which may indeed be based on "hmm, what would I do if I were in a similar situation to the other species".' Maller (2018: 62) argues that these approaches can 'demonstrate how curiosity, caring and empathy can produce different sensibilities to and ways of seeing and knowing the multitudes of non-humans who comprise cities and eco-systems'. This can help rethink cities as habitat for more-than-just-humans, foster understandings of multispecies relationships, who may benefit or be harmed and help to develop more-than-human understandings of cities and processes of urbanisation. Bennett (2015) recognises that the techniques available are not perfect but argues for a sympathy for the suffering of other bodies to further enlightened understandings. Bridle (2022: 76) argues that critical anthropomorphism holds the danger of thinking in human terms by assuming that non-human experience is a poor shadow of ourselves. He suggests that the appropriate question is not 'Are you like us?' But rather 'What is it like to be you?'

This quadrant also raises important issues with regard to material elements. The agency of materials depends on their possibility to adapt or change on the basis of interaction with other elements. Therefore, change of form may also be evidence of a change in agency. For example, storms may be deeper, ice may more often change into water, organisms may mutate and change their characteristics. Information on this is usually derived through the physical sciences and will need to be integrated into any analysis.

Exterior/individual (upper right) quadrant

Wilber labels this the behavioural quadrant and it involves the observation and description of actions and so is easier to undertake in empirical research than the interior quadrants.

For humans, the analysis of behaviour is a commonplace in a number of social sciences and there are many techniques involving direct or indirect observation or self-report to collate the necessary information. The research technique of self-report diaries seems apposite here as a possible source of information on practices as well as the observation of behaviour through video cameras and so on.

Behaviour in individual animals can also be observed. Feeding and reproductive patterns, the way they spend their time, spatial patterns can all be perceived through observation. Information through observation may help to provide understanding of the internal state of the animal. Wilber argues that that there is a link between the internal and external as internal states often have an external manifestation. More cautious behaviour, visible signs of fear or distress, or poor physical health or malnourishment may be signs of internal states.

Behaviour in material elements is usually the focus of the physical sciences and again may be one way of collecting information on the internal state of the organism or material. Does the internal state of the material change during or as a result of performance of the practice?

Interior/collective (lower left) quadrant

Wilber names this quadrant cultural. For humans this involves the taken-for-granted norms of behaviour in society. Analysis of these is the cornerstone of much of sociology and concerned with the formation and maintenance of social norms. A common technique is discourse analysis that may examine the language and forms in which social norms are expressed and justified and their influence on ways of seeing the world and group and societal behaviour.

For animals, the understanding of the concept of what Wilber terms culture may be different. There are clearly behavioural norms, but how they are derived is less clear. Instinct from genetic inheritance and learned behaviour could be said to be an important factor, but there are socialisation practices in many species and behaviour does change according to contextual factors. Ingold (2000) argues that the factors involved are similar between humans and other animals and this may be true particularly for higher level animals as defined by Wilber. For lower level animals (such as those that lack consciousness according to Wilber's definition) there may still be a social structure with a hierarchy including 'leaders' who may set the behavioural standard for others and so the analysis may involve similar elements.

For materials there may be less of a collective culture and the emphasis may be on the use made of them in human and animal cultures. Material 'things' can have important cultural meanings in societies and can reflect and signify important identity and status norms and standings.

Exterior/collective (lower right) quadrant

This quadrant is labelled social by Wilber and involves the observation of collective behaviour.

For humans this involves the behaviour of groups as it shows in the performance of practices. In the field of inhabitation, there may be patterns of behaviour that are common in a particular geographical space or society. Examples may be the choice of owner occupation by many people when they leave the parental home. Of course, these patterns are influenced by all the other quadrants as they may reflect social norms, and individual desires and behaviour. The concept of inhabitation practices, with its basis in structuration theory, captures these interactions well.

Many animals are social creatures and have collective patterns of behaviour. These may be focused around feeding, shelter, as well as reproductive or other forms of behaviour. Materials may also act differently when they are together than when they are apart. For example, the physical action possibilities of one molecule of water may be different than that of an ocean.

Materials, animals (and humans) relate together in social practices and these relationships can shape particular landscapes. The concept of an ecosystem is pertinent here as it charts the interactions and interrelationships and their impacts on the flora and fauna in particular places. However, it must be borne in mind that this quadrant needs to be combined with the others to give a full picture and the constraints of the ecosystem concept discussed earlier need to be borne in mind.

Interactions

Wilber emphasises the importance of taking a holistic perspective and his differentiation into quadrants serves to highlight the areas of analysis that have been ignored or undervalued in previous research. However, one drawback of his approach is that the division into quadrants can hide the interrelationships between them, despite Wilber's attempts to show the links. Wilber discusses the interactions between the quadrants and argues that there are often direct links between them. For example, the interior of an individual human will impact on their behaviour and there will be a similar link at the collective level between social norms and cultures and family and societal behaviours. In the same way, individual behaviour will influence and be influenced by collective behaviour as well as by collective social norms. Making these links is important in engaging with the agency/structure debate that has troubled the social sciences. The concept of inhabitation practices offers a way of doing this through its basis in structuration theory.

In the discussion of the individual quadrants the analysis was divided between human, animal and material elements, largely in order to illustrate the different factors involved in the analysis of each. However, within the holon of an inhabitation practice, there may be substantial interaction between these elements. These interactions may be easier to trace in the right-hand quadrants. For example, the individual and collective behaviour of humans may impact substantially on the behaviour of animals that they are in contact with. If a person leaves out bread for birds then this may change their feeding habits. The behaviour of an animal may also have an impact on human behaviour. For example, the change in feeding habits of foxes may have an impact on the behaviour of humans (and other animals) in a suburban neighbourhood. Also, the existence of some materials may enable humans to perform acts that otherwise would be more difficult or impossible. One person with a shovel or a wheelbarrow or a computer has a different agency than one without those things. The COVID-19 pandemic has highlighted the interactions between viruses and animals and humans. There may also be interactions between the elements on the left-hand interior quadrants. For example, the interior feelings of a human may influence the internal emotions of an animal (such as a horse or household pet) in their presence and of course vice versa. The social norms or cultures of humans may impact on the family and the social life of animals.

Therefore, a major focus on the study of inhabitation practices is on the interactions within and between quadrants as well as on the study of the individual elements involved. Clearly, this may not be an easy task to undertake in a particular research study and may involve a complex and multi-modal research design. This in turn may impact on the choice of inhabitation practice chosen to investigate and the aims of an individual research study and the scale of the analysis employed.

Integration

Although Wilber stresses the interactions between quadrants and the different research traditions and techniques applicable in these quadrants, he has little to say on their integration. A key question is how can information derived from the study of the quadrants and their human, animal and material elements as well as the study of actants and their interactions be reconciled and integrated into a coherent and holistic set of findings? The concept of inhabitation practices gives the framework for this integration to take place, but there will need to be a constant iteration between the different levels of analysis. For example, information on behavioural patterns in the right-hand quadrants will need to be compared with information derived from different techniques in the left-hand quadrants and a reconciliation made between them. In the same way, information from the individual and collective levels will need to be compared and judgement made about the relationship between them.

Nicolini suggests a research strategy for analysing practices should embrace an eclecticism of approaches based on a 'toolkit' of methods. He advocates a pluralist approach in order to provide the 'thicker account of the world we live in' (Nicolini, 2012: 213). His core suggestion is a reiteration of two basic movements: 'zooming in on the accomplishments of practice and zooming out of their relationship in space and time' (2012: 213). He continues:

> [F]irst we zoom in on the details of the local accomplishment of a practice in a specific place to make sense of the of the local accomplishment of the practice and the other more or less distant activities. This is followed by, and alternated with, a zooming out movement through which we expand the scope of the observation following the trails of connections between practices and their products. The iterative zooming in and out stops when we can provide a convincing and defensible account of both the practice and its effects on the dynamics of organising, showing how that which is local contributes to the generation of broader effects. (Nicolini, 2012: 219)

Zooming in involves focusing first on the action or the performance of the practice capturing the 'work' that goes into this:

> Attention should be towards issues such as: What are people doing and saying? What are they trying to do when they speak? What is said and done? How do the patterns of doing and saying flow in time? What temporal sequences do they conjure? With what effect? Through which moves, strategies, methods and discursive practical devices do practitioners accomplish their work? (Nicolini, 2012: 221)

This is accompanied by a foregrounding of the landscape of tools, artefacts and resources, and recording the bodily choreography that goes into accomplishing any practice. Zooming out involves following the associations between different practices and examining how they are kept in place through intermediaries or discursive practices. Also, the focus should be on the results of the practice and how they are used in other contexts.

Evaluation and policy making

One of the advantages of the practices approach is said by Shove et al (2012) to be its importance as a basis for public policy because of its encapsulation of interconnections between human and non-human elements and the structural and agency aspects of any issue. Policy prescriptions that focus on change at the individual level, that is, focus on the need to change individual behaviour, neglect the important structural and material elements that influence this. Maller (2018) shows how the activities of running and walking, which have been shown to increase the health and wellbeing of humans in cities, are practices that are dependent on a range of material elements such as the roads and paths, the presence or absence of trees or animals or even material elements such as mobile phone 'apps'. Also, a sole focus on individual behaviour may neglect the connections with cultural or technical issues. An example may be energy saving in the home. A practices framework allows all of these issues and their interconnections to be considered and a public policy approach adopted that takes them all into account. A key element in policymaking is to be able to evaluate the outcomes of policies and programmes and so an important question here is how this can be achieved using a practices approach whether this is applied at the level of an individual housing programme, housing organisation or at the general level of housing policies. In his discussion of the different elements of the holon, Wilber identified criteria for the quadrants he describes. To recap, he argues that any assessment should include not just the truth of objects, or truthfulness of subjects, or the mesh of intersubjective understanding (justice or rightness), but also the functional fit (mesh of inter-objective relations, 'what does it do?'). The aim of this section is to use Wilber's framework to discuss the evaluation of inhabitation practices. However, it is first necessary to discuss the important concepts of wellbeing and capabilities that have been used in evaluation of housing policies and programmes and briefly referred to in Chapter 1 and other chapters as these two concepts may offer important insights into the evaluation of inhabitation policies and practices.

As outlined in Chapter 1, the concept of wellbeing has been an influential one in housing research as a way of assessing the impact of policies and programmes on the individuals and groups involved (for a review see Clapham et al, 2018). The concept of *objective* wellbeing can be used to measure the exterior elements of a holon as identified by Wilber. At both an individual and collective level, easily collected and standardised measures can be used that give an indication of the state of health of humans. Health may be defined in a narrow way to focus on the lack of physical or mental illness or more broadly to include elements that may be seen to impact on this. In the field of inhabitation these could include activities that can be shown to influence health, such as housing space and other physical conditions, and certain physical and social activities that can be shown to increase health such as social mixing and physical exercise. In general, the concept can be used to provide measures that can be standardised and easily replicated and can provide useful indicators of exterior states. The drawbacks are the partial nature of the indicators as, taken alone, they do not provide insight into the interior quadrants. Nevertheless, it may be possible to make general links between some *objective* indicators and *subjective* states. For example, it may be that some types of physical exercise can increase subjective emotional states and so impact on *subjective* wellbeing or happiness. Another major drawback concerns the choice of indicator to use and who gets to make this choice, which brings with it power to define the objectives of policies and programmes, which is why *subjective* measures that focus on the interior views and states of those involved may be used either in tandem or on their own to overcome this problem. *Subjective* measures of wellbeing usually focus on the end state of 'happiness' and sometimes also on the interior factors that may impact on this such as efficacy and self-esteem. Some of these factors can be reliably measured through the use of standardised indicators and these have even been used to rank countries according to the happiness of their population. The strengths of this approach are that it allows individuals to define their own indicators and that it recognises the importance of changing perceptions and expectations in the measurement of success. *Objective* indicators may be measuring factors that individuals do not value and, therefore, have little influence on their definition of their own happiness or health. However, there may be greater problems with the *subjective* approach in devising easily measurable and reliable indicators and in interpreting them. There are two other important drawbacks of the approach that relate particularly to its use as an indicator of collective interior elements. The first is that it does not move easily from application from the individual to the collective level. The easiest way of achieving the collective measures is to sum the individual ones, but this does not account for the strength of individual views or the question of how to make decisions based on differences. In other words, how are minority views dealt with and what weight is given to them? This issue may be particularly difficult if there are systematic differences between segments of the population such as on social class or ethnicity. Wilber's criterion for the collective interior quadrant is the application of value judgements, which the wellbeing approach does not include. The second problem with the wellbeing approach is that it does not relate to different lifestyles and their valuation by individuals. It is difficult to account for this in the use of indicators of collective wellbeing.

Smith and Reid (2018) argue that the prevalent concepts of wellbeing are based on the assumption of a 'decontextualized and individualized subject' and a view of the self as independent and autonomous. This view has obvious links to the individualism that pervades neoliberal societies and underplays the interpersonal dimensions of reality and the importance of context. They advance an alternative view of a relational concept of wellbeing where it is seen as not being an isolated and discrete phenomenon, but constantly made and remade in interaction with people, materials, animals and places. Practices of everyday life act to give a stabilisation of our sense of self, which allows wellbeing to become stable and meaningful to measure over the medium term. However, the contextualised approach offers a means to understanding how wellbeing can change and provide a guide to the interventions that may facilitate desired change.

The practices approach is well-suited to the analysis of the relational elements that are crucial to the formation of wellbeing. Smith and Reid (2018) argue that this relational view of wellbeing transcends the Cartesian ontological divisions inherent in much of the literature on wellbeing or the 'science of happiness', which focus on the idea of a discrete, sovereign subject at the centre of the social. In the relational view, following the assumptions of the practices approach advocated here, humans are biocultural creatures that are formed by and help to form the context in which they reside.

The concept of capabilities is a useful addition to the tools available to evaluate inhabitation practices. The core claim of the capability approach is that judgements about justice or equality, or the level of development of a community or country, should focus ultimately on the effective opportunities that people have to lead the lives they have reason to value – their capabilities. The key virtue of the capabilities approach is that it accounts for the plurality of goods which individuals have reason to value, including both means (that is, freedoms) and ends (that is, happiness). It accounts for the intrinsic importance of happiness, as having the effective freedom to do the things that one has reason to value will generally enhance one's happiness. But it also accounts for the fact that certain freedoms are right or wrong *regardless* of their consequences. The basis of the approach is a distinction between people's *functionings*, the actions or experiences that people have reason to value, and their *capabilities*, the effective opportunities to achieve these functionings. Through emphasising the latter, the capabilities approach mitigates the risk of paternalism that may be associated with ideas of *objective* wellbeing. To use an example of overcrowding, a family would only be judged impoverished if they did not have the *choice*, or the 'effective freedom', to each have their own room. If the family had sufficient space but just chose not to use it, then we should not consider them to be deprived. By looking at people's *effective freedoms* to have or do things, rather than whether or not they exercise these freedoms, the capabilities approach avoids the imposition of a particular vision of the good life. However, the major problem with this approach is the difficulty in measuring capabilities. In practice, many studies using the capabilities approach are forced, for practical reasons, to use functionings as a proxy for capabilities. Nevertheless, acceptance of the approach does highlight the choice of functionings to be used and how this choice is made, and provides a stimulus for the use of techniques that attempt to examine the effective functionings that people value and are able to adopt. In this way the capabilities approach can relate questions about the evaluation of inhabitation practices to the valued lifestyles of individuals. The concepts of *objective* and *subjective* wellbeing and capabilities can be useful concepts in the evaluation of inhabitation practices. Bearing these in mind, the section continues with a review of the evaluation criteria for the quadrants identified by Wilber.

In his discussion of the different elements of the holon, Wilber identified criteria for the quadrants he describes. To recap, any assessment should include not just the truth of objects, or truthfulness of subjects, or the mesh of intersubjective understanding (justice or rightness), but also the functional fit (mesh of inter-objective relations, 'what does it do?').

Assessment of the right-hand two quadrants is empirically unproblematic. The individual exterior quadrant assessment involves the 'truth' of the observation and in the traditions of science this has been interpreted as concerning replicability and this would seem to be an appropriate criterion here. In other words, would another study using the same methods reach the same conclusions? This may be appropriate for research studies but to analyse the impact of a practice or assemblage on individual behaviour another concept is needed. The concept of capabilities may be pertinent here. In a housing practice the judgement is of the accuracy of the identification of the individual elements of the practice and the function of how they fit together. So, to assess the impact of the practice would involve the identification of its function. In other words, this would be the impact of the interconnections on the behaviour and functioning of the individual holons. For example, one of these could be the functioning of a particular animal species and this could be measured through indicators such as breeding and survival rates and activities such as spread of feeding areas and so on. The concept of *objective* wellbeing may be useful here in identifying appropriate measures. For humans it could be the social practices that are enabled (or made problematic) through particular interconnections. The concept of 'capabilities' may be pertinent here in helping to identify the valued functionings of individuals and collectives.

The collective interior elements involve what Wilber terms 'culture' and he argues that the appropriate assessment criteria involve the use of values. In other words, there is no objective form of evaluation, but they can be judged by comparing actual outcomes with particular valued outcomes. An example could be whether the policies or programmes to be evaluated achieved outcomes that furthered the values of equality or freedom or low carbon use. Clearly the choice and definition of values used in judgement is down to the individual assessor, although there may be techniques that can help to identify shared values within a defined group.

Identification of the interior quadrant of non-human holons or actants is more problematic. It is interesting to speculate whether the human evaluative concepts of wellbeing and culture can be applied to animals. As was noted earlier, there is evidence of meaning and agency in many animals and this should be considered in any evaluation. Although it is difficult to use the human research technique of asking animals, the interior life may be evident through physical or behavioural signs such as of distress. The collective/interior quadrant may be evident in the family and social lives of animals. Changes of behaviour may be evidence of the impact of the practice. As discussed earlier, Maller (2018) argues for the use of an ethnographic sensibility to research with animals and techniques such as critical anthropomorphism (Burghardt, 2007), which can be used to understand complex animal emotional states and ways of being in the world once thought unique to humans, such as the use of tools and other materials in foraging for and consuming food, and attracting mates. However, Ball (2022) cautions against this approach, arguing that the appropriate task is to attempt to understand what it is like to be that creature without ascribing human characteristics. However, it is unclear how humans can do this given that the sensory apparatus and the *Umwelt* may differ extensively. For example, how do humans understand what it is like to be a bat? For other material objects, change of form may also be evidence of a change in agency. For example, storms may be deeper, ice may more often change into water, organisms may mutate and change their characteristics and so on.

The practices approach gives the necessary information for the evaluation of policies and programmes. The holistic analysis of the relationships between the elements in the practice together with an assessment of the agency of the individual elements should enable decision-makers to be able to understand how outcomes are achieved and to identify the key places where intervention can achieve change. The outcomes of a practice can be gauged both on the individual elements of the practice, but also on external factors (such as air pollution levels and so on). Bennett (2015: 86) outlines four steps that can be undertaken in order to understand and intervene in policy problems. The first is to determine the functioning parts of the practice; second, decide which parts are currently the key operators of the practice effects; third, determine which parts are likely to be most susceptible to intervention; fourth, decide what are the best ways to forge a different practice.

From this discussion it is evident that any evaluation of an inhabitation practice, such as a particular policy or programme, will have a number of evaluation criteria as none on their own will capture the important elements involved. The concepts of wellbeing and capabilities can be very useful in the appropriate circumstances but neither will be enough by itself. It will be difficult to combine the different criteria into one overall measure and so decisions will need to be made by considering different measures and making judgements about their relative importance. There is no value-free way to make assessments and the important thing is to make these judgements explicit by making clear the grounds on which they are made and relating them to the objectives to be achieved.

Policy is made within a web of competing interests, perceptions and opinions. The practices framework lays these out for analysis as it unpicks the agents and their actions and relationships that shape policies and programmes. The centrality of power in practices allows policy makers to have a clear idea of the opportunities and barriers to change and lays bare the key points in which intervention may be most effective.

Conclusion

The chapter has shown how the practices approach can be applied by researchers, governments and housing organisations by discussing a general framework that can be fine-tuned to fit the particular circumstances and the resources available. The research approach suggested is complex and involves difficulties in being able to achieve some of the items such as the interior views of animals and materials. However, the importance of taking these factors into account as much as is feasible and appropriate has been stressed. Also, the practices approach provides the information necessary to make a holistic judgement of the outcomes of a policy or programme by suggesting a wide range of assessment criteria, both for the elements of the practice and the outcomes on others, and on the rest of nature, that can be compared with policy objectives and values.

The next three chapters are intended to show the value of the approach to a number of aspects of inhabitation by identifying some of the practices that can impact strongly on the rest of Nature and showing how housing policies and programmes contribute to this.

5

Consumption practices

The aims of this and the following two chapters are to provide examples of the use of the concept of inhabitation practices in order to provide some guidance on the practical use of the concept and to illustrate the contribution that its application can make to the study of inhabitation and to housing policy. Therefore, the aim is not to provide a comprehensive account of research and policy in each area. The scope of the topics covered would make this a difficult enterprise for any one individual to undertake. But, more importantly, the knowledge is not available in many areas to draw any conclusions that would be generalisable in different contexts. Therefore, the aim is to provide examples of the research topics that would be important to pursue, and to provide insight into the methods that could usefully be employed, in the hope that this will inspire the research that will contribute to goals such as climate change and to the health of Nature in general.

In this chapter, the focus is on examples from the consumption of houses and Chapter 6 covers examples from the production process. The following chapter focuses on inhabitation practices outside the home. This division is arbitrary, as will soon become apparent, as the three elements are closely related at many points. It was argued in the previous chapter that the choice of the inhabitation practice to focus on is a subjective one that can be made according to the aims of the particular study and the practical resources of the analyst. Therefore, the division is adopted here as a simplifying mechanism to make the discussion easier to follow. The choice of inhabitation practices to examine in each chapter is meant to show a variety of topics. Some are well covered in housing studies and the aim here is to show the contribution and new insight that the approach can make to traditional concerns of housing policy. However, some of the chosen topics are relatively new to housing studies and here the aim is to increase the scope of the field. Some topics have a strong ecological impact on issues such as climate change or wildlife survival and diversity, but others may not. This is meant to support the contention that the inhabitation practices approach is applicable across the field of housing studies, although the impact will vary according to the particular topic.

It is important to stress that the examples covered here are based on existing studies as the analysis in this book is not based on new empirical research. However, it is hoped that the analysis presented here will stimulate empirical research in the future through the provision of a suitable research framework and the identification of important topics to explore.

Homemaking practices

One of the areas that has received a lot of research attention using a new materialist framework in general and the practices framework in particular is the making of home. The interest has been partly because of the focus on the role of housing in climate change and particularly on the use of energy in the home. The interest is understandable given the policy interest in climate change and the substantial proportion of energy use that takes place in the home, although the precise proportion varies from one country to another. However, as we shall see, the topic is wider than climate change debates and policies, as homemaking practices are at the heart of the consumption of houses and, therefore, of inhabitation and so the topic is important in debates about material use, health and wellbeing and many more vital issues. Despite the new materialist focus on the relationship between humans and material technologies which are at the heart of homemaking practices, much research in this field has been undertaken using a natural science perspective and this has been reflected in the policy focus on the technologies involved. Ellsworth-Krebs et al (2019) criticise the dominance of the building and natural sciences in the research on home comfort and occupant satisfaction that see only the corporeal experiences of thermal comfort and treat it as a measurable and standardised product that can be delivered through technical developments and devices. They point to other social science studies on home comfort that suggest it is a complex phenomenon that has both physical and psychological facets, that meanings are interconnected, and that desires can be contradictory but still valid. They call for more analysis of how energy use relates to ideas of home comfort and the links with practices of homemaking in general.

Where human attitudes and behaviour have been considered in studies of energy use in the home, it has often been assumed that people are 'rational' actors motivated by financial concerns as would be the focus in neoclassical economics. Therefore, it has often been assumed by policy makers that people will react favourably to economic incentives to install energy saving technologies or to reduce consumption. However, as we shall see later, research has shown that people's attitudes and motivations are more varied than this and that some energy reduction programmes have not been as successful as hoped as a result. 'In their efforts to influence homeowners' activities to save energy, policy makers need to consider the broader emotional, social, and cultural meanings of home that influence householders' decisions and everyday life' (Ellsworth-Krebbs et al, 2021: 17). Therefore, the concept of inhabitation practices is of considerable interest and use in this topic because of its focus on the link between material and human elements. As Ellsworth-Krebbs et al note:

> Indeed, the home is an ongoing project, constantly under improvement in response to external changes in technology and ideas of modernity as well as internal shifts related to life course, emotional and financial capacity to make material changes, or negotiate a shared vision with other household members. Home improvements are made in response to aspirations to provide the 'good life' for their family – en-suite bedrooms and enough bathrooms so there are no conflicts with teenagers in the morning, a home office, and big open-plan kitchen – not simply to save energy or improve thermal comfort. (Ellsworth-Krebbs et al, 2021: 17)

It is worth noting the insight of Ingold here that houses and homes are never finished, but constantly made and remade through the practices of inhabitants:

> Building, then, is a process that is continually going on, for as long as people dwell in an environment. It does not begin here, with a pre-formed plan, and end there, with a finished artefact. The 'final form' is but a fleeting moment in the life of any feature, when it is matched to a human purpose, likewise cut out from the flow of intentional activity. (Ingold, 2000: 188)

Therefore, the meaning of the dwelling is not just in the mind of the architect or builder, but is an ongoing project made through the inhabitation practices.

> Yet from a Gibsonian perspective, it is apparent that the world becomes a meaningful place for people through being lived in, rather than through having been constructed along the lines of some formal design. Meanings are not attached by the mind to objects in the world, rather these objects take on their significance – or in Gibson's terms, they afford what they do – by virtue of their incorporation into a characteristic pattern of day-to-day activities. In short, far from being inscribed upon the bedrock of physical reality, meaning is immanent in the relational contexts of people's practical engagement with their lived-in environments. (Ingold, 2000: 168)

Energy efficiency and saving in homes may be offset by the trend in many countries for the increasing size of homes. In order to understand why this is happening it is necessary to examine what people are using homes for. McKinlay et al (2019) suggest that motivation for this trend in house size is the changing sociocultural values on possessions, social status, financial expectations and family life. Others too suggest that fluctuating concepts of family respectability are affecting the size of homes (Dowling and Power, 2012). However, the acceptance of a new large residential norm has consequences for energy use and the rest of Nature.

The use of energy in the home is not an inhabitation practice itself, but it is linked to the project of homemaking and the many inhabitation practices that are involved in this. Homemaking can be usefully seen as a bundle or constellation of individual practices linked by 'connective tissue'. The practices approach has been a popular framework in studies of energy use in the home that wish to move beyond a limited focus on technology and rational consumers. Madsen argues that:

> Practice theory has attracted great interest in the socio-technical research field of energy consumption as an approach that engages with the habitual and mundane practices of the everyday. In this regard, energy consumption is seen as an outcome of these practices (Shove and Walker 2014). Practices are regarded as central to understanding the social world; hence emphasis is on practices such as cooking, cleaning and watching television that are shared across space and time, but performed differently by individuals. Scholars within practice theory and energy consumption studies have established that everyday practices of residents in housing determine to a high degree the energy consumption of a house, or household, as the majority of daily residential routines consume energy. (Madsen, 2019: 330–331)

Homemaking as a practice

Homemaking could be considered to be a bundle of practices that would involve people using material and animal elements to fulfil their conception of what a home consists of. There have been a number of categorisations of what is meant by the concept of home. For example, Somerville (1992) uses six categories of home: shelter; hearth (by which is meant feelings of physical warmth and cosiness); heart (loving and affectionate relationships); privacy (power to exclude others); abode (place to call home); and roots (an individual's source of identity and meaningfulness). This categorisation (and others) could be taken as universal in applying to all or most people in all contexts, however, it is evident that there are strong social pressures in how these concepts are defined by different people in different contexts.

Ellsworth-Krebs et al (2019) identified five physical–psychological home comforts that were commonly identified by householders in their study: relaxation; control; visual comfort; auditory comfort; and familiarity.

Each of these involved interactions between the bodily activities and sensory feelings of humans and material objects:

> Relaxation was the most common synonym for comfort: it was what householders wanted to do in their ideal rooms and what often gave meaning to other desirable aspects of home life. Indeed, participants explicitly connected relaxation with all the other meanings of comfort, except odour and fresh air: tactile (e.g. comfortable seating), visual (e.g. mood lighting as opposed to bright 'task' lighting), familiarity (e.g. having your stuff and usual routines), thermal (e.g. cosy and warm), control (e.g. 'doing what you want'), companionship (e.g. socializing), mental wellbeing (e.g. at ease), physiological (e.g. relaxing with a hot drink or alcoholic beverage), auditory (e.g. listening to music), and contributory comfort (e.g. ensuring guests feel welcomed). (Ellsworth-Krebs et al, 2019: 215)

Madsen stresses the bodily and sensory elements in home comfort:

> Wallenborn and Wilhite (2014) further establish the importance of the body in energy consumption and practice theory, by criticizing the focus on rational and individual behaviour in energy consumption literature. They instead state that the escalating energy consumption can be interpreted as a "transformation of bodies", through practices. In other words, changes in what we perceive as comfort and how we practice our daily lives are inherently bodily (Wallenborn and Wilhite 2014). Thereby, bodies are shaped by practices just as bodies perform and sustain practices. Consequently, comfort is sensed and perceived both bodily and mentally and can be understood as embodied knowhow, bodily sensations and social meanings, for example of home. (Madsen, 2019: 331)

Therefore, the use of energy in the home is perceived as part of the process of the practices of homemaking and the perception of home as sensory environment. This 'sensory home' is seen by Pink (2012) as a way of understanding domestic contexts as intersections of materials and humans, together with discourses of moralities, identities and the sensory, social and material production of a home, through residential everyday activities.

In her research with some relatively affluent Danish homeowners, Madsen concludes that:

> The perceptions of comfort and homeliness were expressed as bodily sensations and social meanings such as warm and cold, well-being and ideas of cosiness. Comfort was experienced as warmth, soft furniture,

relaxation, privacy and also social relations to family. This reflects energy-consuming homemaking practices such as heating, watching television, drinking tea or coffee, showering, and also working from home. ... Homeliness is primarily experienced as the social life of the family, including daily chores of sustaining home and family life as well as things that symbolize this (paintings, books etc.), but homeliness is also experienced as privacy, safety, control and relaxation. This reflects energy consumption in homemaking practices such as cooking, doing laundry, decorating and spending time with the family, for example talking, dining and playing. (Madsen, 2019: 346)

Shove shows how people's expectations of the concept of physical warmth have changed under the influence of changes in technology such as more efficient heating systems or air conditioning and the changing government building standards that influence the built form:

As represented here, the standardisation of comfort is a narrative of ratchet-like path dependency. The conclusions of scientific research are embedded in codes and standards that are in turn reproduced in the built environment and in peoples' expectations of what it should be like. By redesigning homes and offices for air-conditioning, designers have condemned homeowners and workers to an air-conditioned way of life from which there appears to be no way back. Especially not since societies have reorganised around the capacity to manufacture and control conditions inside (whatever the environmental cost). (Shove, 2003: 399)

Also, attention has been focused on other homemaking practices that use energy and attention drawn to other factors that shape outcomes. For example, Shove (2003) has examined the practices involved in laundering clothes and draws attention to the social influences that shape the norms that structure the practices. Her conclusion is: 'All this suggests that contemporary laundry practices (in the UK) are sustained by a distinctive blend of ideas about sensation, display, disinfection, and deodorisation' (Shove, 2003: 402).

In summary, the inhabitation practices approach is of great value in exploring homemaking and consequent outcomes such as energy use. Homemaking can be seen as one practice, or, alternatively, the dwelling can be seen as the location of a bundle of linked inhabitation practices. Examples may be laundry practices, bathing or food preparation, each of which involves the interaction between humans and materials and the use of energy. If the focus is on energy usage, it may be important to break down the usage into the different practices if the aim is to understand trends in overall usage and to form interventions to reduce demand. The different homemaking practices have elements of cooperation, in that they may all rely on ready access to hot water, for example, but may also have competitive elements as they may compete for time or space in the house. Therefore, an increase in overall consumption may involve reductions in the performance of some practices but reductions in others.

Some issues

The research on homemaking practices offers a useful application of the inhabitation practices approach to a topic that is very relevant to debates about climate change. However, existing research needs to be extended if the full insights of the inhabitation framework are to be achieved.

The existing studies examine well the performance of homemaking practices through the interaction between individual humans and the material elements involved in the practice. The focus on the main actors and the qualitative research techniques used have meant that insight has been generated into their interior worlds (the interior/individual quadrant identified by Wilber) as well as the bodily and sensory aspects of performance (the individual/external quadrant). But through this focus a number of general issues have been overlooked in many studies that apply in different ways and to different extents in individual studies. Therefore, what follows are generalisations that apply differentially to particular studies.

First, the studies have been small-scale, qualitative research studies that have small sample sizes in particular locations. This is a very valuable approach that generates many insights as we have seen, but without a large number of studies of different populations in different locations, it is difficult to generalise from the findings. For example, many of the studies have been undertaken with moderately affluent house owners in new or recently upgraded houses. This population would be more likely to be aware of climate concerns and have high competence to perform practices. More studies are needed of renters, less affluent households, different ethnic groups and so on to form a more comprehensive and potentially diverse set of findings that would illuminate the collective/exterior quadrant identified by Wilber through a larger and more representative sample. For example, it has been shown that many renters have different conceptions of home than owners and their control over the technologies to be used may be less. These factors could have large impacts on inhabitation practices and on energy use.

Second, and related to the first point, there is not often a discussion of the aspects of competence. A wider research population would highlight issues of the financial and other resources available and how they impact on the performance of homemaking. For example, there is considerable literature on the meaning of home among renters (see, for example, Soaita and McKee, 2019) and this shows that the context of generally lower incomes and less control over and security in the dwelling can lead to a different conception of home and different elements in its performance. For example, the constrained rights to alter the fabric of the property and the enhanced temporal impermanence and instability of the tenure may result in different inhabitation practices and energy use. Tenants may not have any control over the main energy using equipment. Low-income families may be unable to enjoy some homemaking practices to the extent that others can and may have different practices because of inability to afford materials such as insulation or efficient heating sources that may reduce energy consumption.

Third, there has been an over-focus on one person in the household and a lack of concern with negotiations by members of the household on practices. For example, are there differences in the desired temperature within the house? Who performs in the practices and where more than one person is involved are there differences in performance? This relates to the debate about the appropriate level of analysis in housing studies as the individual or the household. If the latter is taken (which may be appropriate in many cases) the interactions involved in making decisions and in the performance of practices need to be examined as they may be important elements in the practice.

Fourth, there is an absence of animals in consideration of the household. Despite the lack of attention, domestic pets consume food, use space in the house, are washed and have wishes that relate to heating levels in the home. Pets inhabit many homes as members of the household, although the rights and duties this involves and the practices that they participate in may vary depending on the particular species and the orientations of the other members of the household as well as the physical structure of the house. At least pets need to be incorporated as an element in household inhabitation practices in order to generate insight into the nature of these practices. However, it may be possible to go further. In previous chapters we have discussed the idea that animals can be the focus in defining and examining inhabitation practices and it may be worthwhile to test out this proposition as a way of gaining further insight into their place in the home and its impact on environmental and other issues.

Fifth, although there has been a focus on some major technological materials such as heating systems, there has been a lack of focus on the smaller-scale materials involved such as soaps and other cleaning materials. They have an embodied energy and may contain constituents that impact on the body of the user, the environment within the house and outside it. Also, they will carry significance in terms of meaning and identity which are made and reinforced through product design and marketing activity. The focus in many of the studies has been on energy use, but the inhabitation practices examined may have other important impacts, such as on biodiversity. For example, the increased use of cleaning materials in the performance of bathing and cleaning practices may impact on the organisms in the house. The attitude of actors towards them may be influenced by ideas of comfort and cleanliness that underpin the practices. The absence or presence of certain organisms such as bacteria and viruses may impact on the health of the house members either positively or negatively. The presence of harmful viruses (such as COVID-19) may impact negatively, but there is increasing concern that the extermination of many bacteria may be having an impact on the health of people's immune systems. Also, many cleaning products may have an impact on the air quality in the house.

There has been little focus on the materials used in the artefacts involved in furnishing a house. Homemaking for many people includes decorating, hanging paintings and buying curtains, carpets and other floor coverings and furniture such as tables, chairs and so on. Dominant discourses and norms of appropriate design will influence these homemaking practices and the interests of manufacturers and designers may be to propagate a throw-away culture that encourages frequent remodelling and renewal with the resultant resource use. As another example, the use of lighting may be an important element in interior design that may influence energy use. Design ideas or discourses may be important 'connective tissue' in linking many homemaking practices.

Because of the focus on energy use in the home there has been a lack of analysis of the wider impact of homemaking practices on issues other than carbon emissions and climate change. For example, we have already mentioned the lack of concern with the embodied energy in materials used such as washing soaps, showers and so on. Biodiversity issues have also been relatively neglected. A holistic analysis of the impact of homemaking practices would examine the whole impact on the health and wellbeing of the occupants as well as the wide impact on the rest of Nature.

Sixth, the layout and size of the house is an important factor in the performance of some practices. For example, the increased incidence of bathing, combined with changing ideas of privacy and comfort, has been linked with an increase in the number of bathrooms in houses. The design of bathrooms has reflected different bathing practices (such as showers rather than baths) as well as changing ideas of style and status. In other words, bathing practices influence the number, size design, layout and style of the bathroom just as this in turn influences bathing practices in a reciprocal relationship. Therefore, the production and design of houses needs to be cognisant of homemaking practices just as the practices are influenced by the design and materials used in the production of the house. These examples illustrate the important links between the consumption of houses through homemaking practices and their production which will be considered in Chapter 6.

Seventh, the small-scale and ethnographic nature of many of the studies has restricted the analysis of the structural factors or connective tissue that impact on inhabitation practices. For example, a number of studies have been aware of the collective norms and understandings of factors such as cleanliness or comfort (Wilber's collective interior quadrant), but have not examined the factors that influence them beyond the performance of practices. The essence of the practices approach is the link between agency and structure and so any study needs to be aware of both elements. It may be difficult to include an in-depth analysis of both in an individual research study, given resource constraints and the emphasis in academic publishing on short journal articles. Therefore, in order to gain a comprehensive picture, there may be a need for a series of studies that examine different aspects of an issue or practice and follow through on the structural elements. It is important to 'zoom out', as discussed in the previous chapter, in order to capture these and to understand fully the factors that influence the performance of the practice and its outcomes.

Eighth, there has been little consideration of the practices of the creation and maintenance of the immediate environment of the house. This space may be maintained by individual households or by collectives of one kind or another. Legal and other rights and obligations over the space may differ. The size and form of the spaces may vary. Some will be internal to a building and others in the open air. Some may be covered with materials such as concrete, gravel or paving slabs, others may be cultivated whether laid to lawn, or used to grow flowers for decoration, or vegetables for eating, or any combination of these. For some people, a space such as a garden may be an important part of the home space and its upkeep may be considered to be an important homemaking practice and is, therefore, worthy of study. Also, the nature and upkeep of this space may have important implications for climate change or biodiversity as we shall argue later in the chapter.

Ninth, there has been little consideration of the inhabitation practices of those without a settled home such as those categorised as homeless or those who spend at least some time sleeping rough or on the streets. There has been research on the situation of people in this context, as we shall see in the next section, but little has used the practices framework. We shall explore in the next section how the concept of inhabitation practices can add value to the study of homelessness.

In summary, studies adopting the principles of new materialism and in particular the practices approach, have shed considerable light on homemaking practices and, in particular on energy use in the home that could have important impact on policy designed to ameliorate climate change. However, existing studies taken collectively have a number of shortcomings, identified earlier, that mean that the approach has yet to deliver its full potential. To illustrate this, the following sections will examine two areas not fully covered in existing research and highlighted in this section.

The first is homemaking practices performed by people without a settled home. The second is gardening practices.

Homemaking practices without a settled dwelling

There has been a considerable volume of research on homelessness in many different countries and contexts (for a review see Fitzpatrick, 2012). Some studies have focused on the causes of homelessness and the impact of policy responses to it, including different statutory provisions and institutional responses. Other studies have focused on the everyday experience of homeless people themselves. The concept of a homeless pathway has sometimes been used to bring these elements together (Clapham, 2003).

There has been an ongoing concern about the health of homeless people, the detriment to health caused by rough sleeping and the lack of access to health services that can result from homelessness. The COVID-19 pandemic has given an added impetus, but also a different focus to some of these discussions. For example, in England the government provided funding to remove many homeless people from the streets because of the perceived threat to their health and to the health of the population at large from the pandemic. This help was time-limited, but it did show to many people that rough sleeping could be overcome with the appropriate political will, but the episode also shows the health and wellbeing issues associated with the phenomenon. Another aspect of the situation was the perception of the health risk of communal living environments such as hostels (Fitzpatrick et al, 2021). There were arguments that communal living exposed residents to risk of the virus and added to existing critiques of these forms of provision that had focused on the lack of facilities and the difficulties of homemaking in that context, including issues of privacy, stability and security.

The COVID-19 situation has illustrated the importance of using the inhabitation practices approach to examine the holistic circumstances of rough sleeping or hostel living, in a way that sheds light on the material and animal elements of the situation as well as the human ones. Sleeping on the streets can be viewed as an inhabitation practice that involves a number of elements. The rough sleeper has competencies that enable them to perform in the practice that may include emotional and health resources as well as knowledge of the safest or driest places to sleep. These competencies will be strongly influenced by structural issues of inequality that result in patterns of educational achievement and health status. The rough sleeper will have expectations of what are the important aspects of a suitable home that will be influenced by dominant discourses. Other humans will be participants in the practice, whether other rough sleepers, police and security officers, and users of the street such as shoppers and so on. Interactions between them will be shaped by discourses and norms of behaviour that may influence the expectations of rough sleepers and the desirability and impact of the practice. These may be formalised in laws or guidelines that shape behaviour in certain situations. The material elements of the practice may involve the available resources to create a shelter as well as the nature of any resting place. Some potential places have been deliberately shaped in order to deter their use for rough sleeping through the installation of spikes or barriers. Each place will have its own material make-up that will influence the practice and offer different levels of comfort and safety to the rough sleeper. Also, the material element of the place will provide the environment for animals. Relevant ones would include the micro-organisms that can result in disease such as COVID-19 as well as a host of others such as stray dogs that may also inhabit the site and wild animals such as foxes or snakes depending on the context. The rough sleeper may have a pet dog that is an important part of their life, providing company and affection as well as possibly increasing a sense of security and home.

The same analysis of the homemaking practice can be made of different forms of accommodation such as a hostel or temporary bed and breakfast rooms. The forms that homemaking practices take in these different settings can be taken as an assessment of the quality of accommodation using the capabilities framework as a guide as was outlined in the previous chapter.

Gardening practices

The inhabitation practices that are sited in the space immediately outside a dwelling may vary considerably depending on the nature of this space. For some people that live in apartments it may consist entirely of a view that they cannot physically enter or a small balcony. For others living in houses, the space may be extensive and offer opportunities for many practices that may involve socialising or growing flowers or vegetables or keeping animals. There are differences between cultures and climates in the extent to which space is considered to be 'outside' as the practices of home may be performed there that in other cultures and situations would be undertaken indoors. The barriers between the inside and the outside may be material or social and vary in their permeability. The distinction between private and public outdoor space may vary in the same way and the rights of access that people have may be individual or collective and could vary considerably. For some people the performance of practices in this outdoor space may be an important element in their homemaking and be an important way in which they interact with the rest of nature. Gardening is a common pastime in many cultures as is the keeping of pets. Looking out onto a green space may be important to people's wellbeing.

However, in the planning and building of houses the outdoor space seems to get less consideration than the indoor space and concerns about it tend to be reduced to questions related to urban density (see the next two chapters for a further discussion of this). High density, with a corresponding small outdoor space, is often thought of as being more 'sustainable' because of the reduction in travel that denser cities may bring about. But outdoor space may have considerable benefits to individuals and to the rest of nature, although this may depend on the practices undertaken there. The physical nature and layout of spaces may vary and this may be linked to the practices and their impacts. For example, if a space is devoted to the parking of cars and is paved over, there may be impacts on rainfall runoff and on the flora and fauna. Alternatively, the space may be used to grow vegetables for food, or be grassed over for exercise of animals or humans, and be planted to encourage other animals such as birds or bees, or with plants such as trees that will capture carbon.

Maller views gardening as:

> [A] complex of connected and co-dependent practices that include sowing and cultivation of seeds and cuttings, bed preparation and soil management, pruning, watering, harvesting, pest management and killing. Many of these practices would share elements such as competencies in how to use tools and handle plants, meanings about when and why specific practices should be carried out and the sequence, and various materials and equipment, such as gloves, clippers, fertilizers, buckets, rakes and wheelbarrows. (Maller, 2018: 118)

Gardening practices may vary according to the objectives of the gardener and may have very different impacts on humans, animals and materials. Maller (2018) differentiates between productive gardening (for food), wildlife gardening and therapeutic gardening. The practices of gardening will be shaped by climate, culture and individual taste and may vary widely. Some gardeners will plant flowers that are not indigenous to the area and place them in an order based on shape or colour and different flowering times so that there is colour in the right place at the right time. Indigenous and wild plants will be classed as weeds and removed. Some animals such as birds or squirrels may be encouraged into the space through feeders, while others, such as slugs or rabbits, are excluded as pests. Garden areas may be set aside for household pets that may influence the flora and the other animals that may be excluded from this space. Barriers may be erected to exclude unwanted elements of 'nature'. Trees and hedges will be trimmed and shaped. Grass lawns will be regularly watered and mowed during the summer months. Alternatively, some may see themselves as the guardians of the local landscape and 'wild' their gardens by using indigenous wild flowers, leaving unkempt areas and planting native trees and plants that encourage wildlife. All forms of gardening involve 'relations and entanglements between humans and non-humans' (Maller, 2018: 119). Gardening practices involve many elements such as plants, insects, solar energy, water, micro-organisms, soil and nutrients, in which the processes involved are shaped by the different agencies of the elements in a dynamic co-performance. The performance of these practices can impact on the liveability (for humans and animals) and biodiversity of urban (and rural) environments.

Pitt (2014) argues that gardens have been perceived as 'therapeutic places' that improve wellbeing, but that this concept ignores the possible negative or stressful feelings that gardens may stimulate in some people and in some circumstances. For example, the necessity to keep them tidy may be stressful for those without the resources, physical capability or motivation to do this. Pitt argues that places are not necessarily therapeutic because of their intrinsic attributes, rather wellbeing is created through the interplay of people and the place in particular forms of socio-natural engagement in 'dynamic co-performance' (Maller, 2018). In their study of community gardens, Pitt (2014) found that gardeners mentioned the activity involved in gardening as being therapeutic in that it encouraged an active engagement with nature that focused attention away from troubling thoughts and worries. Pitt uses the concept of 'flow' to describe how bodily movement of gardeners brought about ease and enhanced therapeutic feelings. Gardens were seen as more likely to lead to therapeutic feelings as they were seen as places different from everyday routine environments. Feelings of belonging and control were said to be important in generating 'flow'.

Gardening practices raise some interesting issues about the way that 'nature' is perceived and valued. Some categories of gardening can be perceived as ordering or domesticating nature and moving away from nature perceived as a wild or unstructured or even threatening force. There is an interesting theme in writing by Macfarlane (2007) and others about the cultural perception of wildness or wilderness and how mountains have been sometimes perceived as ugly and threatening and at others picturesque and sites for contemplation and recreation. There is a substantial literature on the restorative effect of 'nature' but in the Anthropocene, where all landscapes are affected by humans in one form or another, it is unclear what is meant by nature here as is explored in more detail in Chapter 7 where the practices of leaving the home to visit 'nature' are discussed. A number of questions are important here. What is it about 'green places' or nature that offers restoration? What elements of a garden are people trying to create? Is nature being domesticated in the sense of being seen as part of homemaking?

The questions are important to generate an understanding of how people perceive outdoor spaces, what they mean to them and what they are trying to achieve through managing them. The inhabitation practices approach offers an important technique for examining these issues. It enables the focus to include the outside and the environs of the house as well as the inside and provides a holistic research framework that examines the different aspects (or quadrants) of the human, material and animal elements of practice and their interactions. In addition, it can lead to an examination of the context within which inhabitation practices are performed. Insight would also be generated by placing animals and minerals at the centre of practices. For example, the focus on an animal could elucidate the impacts of different gardening practices on the animal practices and could impact on its wellbeing. The analyses outlined here can further understanding of homemaking practices and of the function that houses perform for people, but also for helping to understand the myriad links between these everyday practices and the rest of Nature that impact on issues such as climate change.

Homemaking practices and policy

The primary contribution of the practices approach to policymaking is the insight to be gained from analysis and understanding of the web of human, material and animal factors that lead to particular outcomes. This knowledge should enable policy makers to design interventions that are effective in generating the required change. For example, Shove (2003) has argued that the practices approach moves beyond a policy focus on individual behaviour and gives a much more comprehensive picture of the situation that should allow for policy interventions that are sensitive to the factors involved and their interactions. Horne (2018: 188) uses the example of showering to make a general point about the need to consider wider factors than individual human behaviour and to tailor interventions to both practices and how the elements of practices are constituted: 'Targeting showering requires targeting the changing meanings of showering and how these are being reframed, requiring targeting those agencies that are trying to promote more hot water use or are doing so inadvertently through their actions.'

The need for a better conception that underlies policy is made by Horne (2018: 64) who draws attention to the lack of impact of policy: 'GHG (greenhouse gas) emissions resulting from energy use in residential buildings have continued to rise despite global attempts to set binding policies to reduce carbon emissions and climate mitigation and energy efficiency policies targeting cities, houses and households.' Horne cites many reasons for this, among which was changes in housing arrangements:

> Although average energy used by OECD households fell from 1971 to 2001, at the same time residential energy demand increased 32 per cent (OECD 2003). The fall in average energy used was due mainly to building efficiency upgrades, while the rise in energy demand was due to declining household sizes as people moved away from larger households to live alone or with one other person, resulting in a 36

per cent increase in the number of dwellings. At the same time, total energy consumed for lighting and by appliances rose 70 per cent despite more energy efficient lighting because the total number of lights, levels of illumination and lighting technologies increased. (Horne, 2018: 65)

Therefore, energy use was impacted considerably by mainstream housing policies as well as homemaking practices. Maller et al (2012) found that green renovations were ineffective in reducing households' energy consumption, precisely because these often conflicted with everyday practices and notions of the ideal home. The impact of energy saving renovations was often offset by, for example, owners increasing floor space, and adding kitchen extensions and bathrooms (Maller et al, 2012). In this way, the construction of comfortable homes that are also energy-efficient needs to account for everyday practices, bodily sensations of comfort and sociocultural notions of home.

Ellsworth-Krebbs et al (2021) argue that the research findings on energy use reveal some potential strategies to reduce energy demand: such as beginning to challenge social perceptions that bigger homes are always better; questioning the need for guest bedrooms and how the 'peak household' is accommodated; and supporting initiatives and policies that encourage and enable householders to downsize. They argue that intervening in the trend towards smaller households and under-occupation of homes is arguably a more significant way to reduce demand per person than upgrading a boiler or loft insulation. They conclude that: 'Thus, this suggests avenues of research that could challenge the processes by which shared expectations are generated, rather than relying on improvements in efficiency to reduce energy demand, such as investigating how privacy and personal space is negotiated in smaller dwellings and by different cultures' (Ellsworth-Krebs et al, 2021: 16). Widening the scope of analysis involved in the making of housing policy through adoption of the inhabitation practices framework shows the interconnections that shape what are often perceived as individual housing issues such as energy use. Adoption of the framework brings into consideration the wide variety of factors that impact on energy use, which opens up wider housing consumption and policy issues. It raises questions about the factors that shape the current pattern of consumption in housing and asks why people want larger houses that use more energy.

The potential for policy change is not just confined to the energy-saving field. Homemaking practices lie at the heart of many of the issues that have traditionally been the concern of housing policy. For example, homemaking practices are ways in which households seek to improve their health and wellbeing. Therefore, the ability to achieve desired practices in a particular dwelling is an important element of housing quality. The discussion earlier in the chapter on the impact of different settings on homemaking practices could form the basis of a measure of housing quality. Rather than a sole focus on the physical aspects of a dwelling, a focus on practices would lead to a recognition of what a house does for people, in terms of enabling them to achieve their desired practices. The practice approach marries well with the capability approach to the evaluation of policy as discussed in earlier chapters.

The ability of a household to undertake desired homemaking practices is an important capability that underpins many other aspects of life. Therefore, it is an important element of inequality and offers a perspective in which to undertake policy to deal with housing disadvantage and inequality. The ability of a household to perform in a homemaking practice may depend on a number of factors as we have discussed in the chapter. One factor may be the competence of the household to perform in the practice that may be influenced by their knowledge, physical or mental abilities or financial and other resources. Differences in the physical and sensory home environments may make the performance of a practice more or less difficult. Other material, human and animal elements involved in the practice may also have an influence. Analysis of these factors and their interaction at an individual and collective level may provide important information in the making of a policy.

Conclusion

In this chapter applications of the practices approach to housing consumption have been reviewed. It has been argued that the existing studies have shown the potential value of the framework on issues such as energy use in the home through analysis of the practices of showering or heating. The practices approach shows the important interactions between the human, animal and material elements that constitute a practice, including the connective tissue such as the technologies and discourses that shape many different practices. However, the chapter has shown that there are a number of weaknesses that stem from the limited scope of the studies and has described ways that these problems can be overcome.

Two illustrations of inhabitation practices involved in consumption have been given here, namely the homemaking practices of people without a settled home and gardening practices. The former shows the importance of animal and material elements in a traditional topic of housing research and highlights the value of incorporating these elements into any analysis through the practices approach. The discussion of gardening practices extends previous analyses of homemaking practices by including the space around the house as a locale of home. Practices in the garden (or outside space where no garden exists) are linked to those inside the house and have important impacts on the rest of Nature.

The chapter concludes with a discussion of the role of the practices approach in providing information for the policymaking process. It is argued that unpicking the human, animal and material elements of a practice and their interactions provides an understanding of the important ways that policies can be designed in order to achieve desired changes. Inhabitation practices offer an important focus for the achievement of change that could have a profound impact on some aspects of Nature such as energy and material usage as well as biodiversity.

6

Production practices

As noted earlier, most studies of practices have focused on consumption, as witnessed in the specific field of inhabitation by the research on housing consumption through homemaking practices discussed in Chapter 5. However, as was argued in Chapter 3, there is no reason why the practices approach cannot be applied to the production of housing and generate important insights that may be relevant to housing outcomes and policy concerns. The importance of the topic has been recognised in the studies of energy use in the home because of the realisation that the built form locks in future energy use. Horne (2018: 2) argues that: 'Houses are obdurate structures, yet they are constantly being remade and reformed. Form and fabric are significant investments that, once made, tend to "lock in" future energy use throughout occupation of a dwelling.' Also, the building of houses involves substantial embodied energy in materials and construction, although, as Horne points out, this is only small proportion (10–20 per cent) of total energy usage during the lifetime of a home as measured through life-cost accounting (LCA). However, as higher standards of energy efficiency in use are achieved, this proportion could increase to 40–60 per cent, which is said to be the current norm for high energy, low energy use buildings today (Horne, 2018). Imrie (2021) argues that the construction industry has the world's largest ecological footprint and impact by using materials like concrete with high levels of embodied energy. He further argues (2021: 32): 'Building is a disruptive and violent process, ranging from the destructive extraction of non-reproducible materials from the earth, to the colonisation of land from nature, and disturbance of socio-ecological systems.' Imrie (2021) also argues that much new construction is inappropriate because it does not enable the stability of settlement (or inhabitation in the terminology used in the book) particularly because of its relationship to the environment in which it is often placed such as in areas at high risk of floods or fires and the encroachment of building into the edges of wild areas with the increased risk of disease. He argues (2021: 20) that the aim should be 'the creation of nurturing and life affirming spaces integral to the health and wellbeing of people and nonhuman species' but that current practices mean that this is rarely achieved.

The structure and practices of the house-building industry in many countries have been widely criticised. It has been characterised as a diverse sector that is resistant to change and so is reliant on traditional forms of organisation and depends on the learned skills of individuals in the workforce, often operating on the construction site. It has been argued that the sector in many countries is unaware of its impact on the rest of Nature and is a major contributor to changes in climate and habitat, while being resistant to the adoption of 'green' measures. Applications of the practices approach to production processes should enable the relationships and actants to be identified that shape housing outcomes and provide information that is relevant to policy making.

The lack of previous research using the practices framework means that the approach in this chapter will be different from the discussion of consumption in the previous chapter as there is not enough material to provide a review of existing studies and their strengths and weaknesses. Instead a general review of the production process is given to provide the context for the overall discussion. Although the process may be different in the different tenures because of the role of government and other agencies may vary, the focus here is on the production of private sector owner occupied sector which in most countries provides most new housing construction. Nevertheless, the approach can be utilised in all sectors and tenures.

The chapter then focuses on three topics within the production process in order to give indications of how the approach can be applied and the value of the analysis. The first focus is on the house-building site as the location where the practices involved in the production process come together as the house is constructed. This focus can provide a way in to analysis of the individual practices that contribute to the whole. The second focus is on the organisational and professional practices that are pursued by the many organisations and professions that are involved in house production, including trades such as plumbers or electricians and professions such as surveyors, town planners and so on working for many different kinds of organisations. The third focus is on the discourses that can be viewed as 'connective tissue' that link many individual practices by providing the context for their performance. The chapter concludes with a discussion of some of the policy issues that are raised by the analysis of production practices, focusing on the impacts on the rest of Nature.

The practices of house building

The practices of new house building involve the conversion of the inputs of land, labour, materials, finance and technical expertise into the output of houses. This is often divided into practices of project conception and evaluation, land preparation, building construction, and marketing and sales (Clapham, 2019), each of which could be divided further into many individual practices. The practices are constituted through the interaction of actants and structure, and both elements can be multifaceted in house building. For example, many different professionals are involved in the practices such as architects, surveyors, engineers, town planners, accountants and so on, and each has its own set of beliefs and practices. Many different skills such as plumbing or electrical work can be involved with different sets of knowledge bases and working practices. Many different private, state and community agencies may be part of the process, each with its own organisational culture and practices. Some may be focused on profit-making and derive these from particular parts of the supply process such as the accrual of land value or the production process itself. Some public sector organisations may have a different set of organisational goals that may be focused on house-building targets or affordability criteria. Governments at many levels may be involved in the process for different political objectives. There may be systematic differences between countries in the organisation of the house supply process depending on geography, political culture, industrial organisation and type of housing as well as different forms of organisation meeting niches or market positions within each country.

From this discussion it is evident that it could be very difficult to define a generic practice or set of practices that is generally relevant across space and time. The discussion also highlights the complexity of any attempt to construct individual practices at any scale. Added to these problems can be the difficulty of gaining research access to some organisations because of perceived privacy and confidentiality considerations. For example, some organisations may be concerned about commercial secrecy issues that they may think threaten their commercial survival or success.

The difficulties outlined perhaps explain why there has been less research on production practices than in the consumption sphere. The strategy that will be pursued in this chapter is to examine existing evidence and try to construct an overall picture of the inhabitation practices involved in house production by focusing on the three different aspects already outlined. The first is to focus on the building site as the location where the different practices converge in shaping the final product and provides a way to identify the different practices involved and their relationships.

The house-building site

The building site is where the various elements that make up the inhabitation practice of new house building come together and so is a useful place to start in the unpicking of the elements. Mapping the interactions of the actants is a useful starting point in identifying the elements and relationships that shape the final form of the house and its place in Nature. The main human actors in this situation are the building workers as well as the providers and deliverers of the raw materials used and those overseeing the process, whether project managers, building control officers, architects or town planners. The individual and collective actions will be influenced by the beliefs, knowledge and training of those involved (their competencies) and the way that these are formed can be traced back to their background, education, training and the discourses that shaped the practices that they are socialised into. The interactions between actors will be orchestrated by formal and informal rules that may influence who does what and the extent and influence of different roles. The tasks that need to be undertaken on site will vary depending on the extent of pre-fabrication of the building constituents. If this is pursued to any great extent, it may be that the factory can be viewed as a key locale of construction as well as the traditional building site. The primary focus in previous studies of the impact on building houses on the rest of Nature has been on the construction materials used. These will have been stipulated off-site by architects, planners and other building technicians, and this is an important strand to uncover. Why are certain materials such as concrete widely used despite their high levels of embodied energy and their constitution of finite materials? Some materials such as windows or paints may use oil in their construction as well as materials in short supply and may have embodied energy. Other materials such as sand or aggregate also use up energy in their extraction and transportation to the construction site. These materials are finite, although it may seem as though there is enough to meet demand at the moment, although others such as oil may be closer to levels considered to be problematic.

The location where minerals are extracted is also an important site to study as part of the house-building process as the removal of matter and the construction of buildings and access roads will have had an impact on the humans, animals and materials that occupied this site and the surrounding area. Animals may have had to change their inhabitation practices and vegetation will have been destroyed. The process of extraction will create noise and dust that may impact on animals and humans. The transportation to the construction site will probably use fossil fuels as well as creating noise and atmospheric pollution for those living close to the roads or tracks used. The use of timber as a construction material will have involved the felling of trees and the changing of landscapes and habitats. If not replaced, there will be an impact on carbon capture in the environment. In summary, the focus on the inhabitation practices of the construction site offers an opportunity to trace the materials used both in terms of why and how they were chosen as well as their impact on the form that the house takes, but also the impact this has on the rest of Nature.

Shove (2017) categorises three roles of materials in practices as being: resources consumed in the practices (which we have focused on so far in the discussion); infrastructure that are necessary for performance of the practices, but are not related to them directly (an example may be the office premises of the architects or other professionals); materials used at the construction site, which may be important elements of the inhabitation practice because of their use by humans as devices in the construction process. For example, machinery such as cranes, saws, piledrivers and drills enable humans to perform tasks that would be more difficult or impossible to do without them and so have an important impact on the costs of construction and the form that a house takes. However, they also have used materials and energy in their manufacture and in their use. Other material phenomena may be used in the design process and so also influence the form of the house. For example, much design is undertaken with the use of computer software that because of the processes and practices installed will shape the design and form of the house. Computers use energy in their construction as well as being constituted of finite materials, some of which are scarce and demand considerable resources to extract and refine them.

The animal elements of the inhabitation practice of the building site are mainly those living in the near location and on the site itself. The construction process may start with site preparation that may involve clearance of the land through the removal or movement of soil and vegetation that may form the habitat of a number of species of animals as well as the plant life itself. Site preparation may involve demolition of existing buildings.

Imrie criticises the lack of attention to the building site within the culture of building practices. He argues:

> The culture of building rarely encourages its practitioners to think about a building site as a vital, living organism, or part of a broader, holistic environment that has intrinsic value, or a value in itself, for itself. Rather, landscapes and ecologies tend to be regarded as just another resource to be costed or factored into a cost calculus as part of the broadcloth of a construction project. (Imrie, 2021: 342)

He argues that the result is 'to insert a building into a place, without any connection to the setting, or sensitivity to the ecological fabric' and that this 'undermines one of people's primary needs, for ongoing connections with the natural world' (Imrie, 2021: 342).

Imrie's critique of the outcome of building practices poses the question of how they should be evaluated by rejecting the argument that Nature is a resource to be used by humans and placing emphasis on the wellbeing of animals and materials and their capabilities as discussed in Chapter 4.

This brief overview of some aspects of the building process and its location on the building site show the value of its use as a starting point for the analysis of inhabitation practices. The way that the different human, animal and material elements interact gives important insight, both into the process of house construction, but also the shape and impact of the final product of the dwelling itself. Analysis of the interactions at the location of the building site offer the opportunity to trace the factors that have influenced the actions and interactions, whether professional or organisational ideologies or practices, political discourses, material technologies, or animal and material feelings and behaviours. Some of these elements are discussed in the following sections.

Organisational and professional practices

The complexity of the housing development process has already been highlighted. Many different professions and occupations are involved and each has its own set of working practices, ideologies and beliefs that may overlap or be different from those of others. In addition, a number of organisations are involved and each of these may have its own working practices. Nicolini (2012) conceptualises organisations as bundles of practices that are both the site and the result of work activities. Countries differ in the organisation of their housing development process and even within individual countries there may be differences between small and large house-builders, for example, that may operate within specific market niches and have working practices attuned to their situation. Horne (2018) sees builders as the centre of a web of organisations that includes materials manufacturers and suppliers as well as exchange professionals such as estate agents, and building professionals such as surveyors, engineers and architects. There are many forces that may lead to differentiation within the house-building sector, but also factors that encourage similarity. Horne (2018) points to the industry associations that encourage 'good practice', set training and education syllabuses and accredit professional courses in Australia and many other national contexts.

Horne (2018) argues that the house-building industry in general is wedded to traditional working practices and is resistant to change. He sees this as a major reason why attempts by many governments to reform the industry and its working practices have been limited in their success and why the sector has not been successful in reducing its energy use to any substantial degree. Shove et al show how the complexity of the interlinked practices can hinder change by discussing the example of the introduction of reinforced concrete as a building material:

> Before reinforced concrete could be adopted as normal, many people had to become familiar with its qualities and with the conditions and circumstances of its effective use. This was especially challenging in that the properties of concrete differ from one batch to the next because of the variable nature of the materials involved and the conditions in which they are mixed and applied. In the early days concrete expertise was craft-based, embedded and locally reproduced. As knowledge of the material became more widely shared it also (and in the same move) stabilized to the point that it could be defined, taught and learned

regardless of the situation. Subsequent developments in standard specifications and regulations have the further effect of stabilizing what counts as expertise and of shaping both the nature of reinforced concreting and the first-hand experience-based competencies of those involved. (Shove et al, 2012: 50)

The example of reinforced concrete shows that change in the practices of house building can be achieved through a number of actants (in this case through technical change in materials) but can require acceptance from a number of different agents (some of whom may find their existing expertise challenged or becoming redundant) and changes in a number of working practices, which may explain why change can be slow.

Imrie (2021) decries the instrumentalist rationality that, he argues, is at the heart of building practice. One aspect of this is that material and animal aspects of Nature are regarded as resources to be used when it is profitable and useful to do so. Imrie (2021: 323) points to a 'culture that is wedded to the belief in technology to overcome the limits to building, by providing a constant supply of new techniques to control nature, and to rework it into new, often synthetic products'. He points to the widespread use of plastics as a laboratory-engineered material that is used in every part of a building, but whose longevity and resistance to recycling will leave a 'toxic legacy' for a long time to come.

Another aspect of the instrumentalism inherent in the approach by the house-building industry, that is enshrined in its working practices, is an approach to valuation that stresses monetary value as the way of evaluating action. As we pointed out in Chapter 1, this approach fails to account for factors other than market value, such as the impact on Nature. This approach is enshrined in the working practices of the valuation of land and other assets by valuers and surveyors. As Imrie (2021) points out, it is this approach that leads to the search for increased monetary value through demolition of existing housing and rebuilding to increase the monetary returns and increase land value. For example, the demolition of council estates in London has been well documented (see, for example, Watt, 2021). The impetus here has been to replace low yielding assets (for example, council housing in need of repair and renewal but let at relatively low rents) with new owner-occupied apartments that can yield a higher monetary return and increase the market value of the land. In turn, this approach reinforces a culture of demolition of existing houses without consideration of the social or environmental costs. As Imrie states:

As much as we build we demolish and destroy, and building cultures are defined, in part, by the tendency towards obsolescence of products and objects, and the restless urge to renew and reconstruct. The sounds and sights of demolition are ever present, ranging from the visibility of wrecking machinery to the production of rubble dust and dirt in the atmosphere. The effects are irrational, often disruptive, and include the loss of scarce materials; the increase in waste and landfill; particulate and noise pollution due to demolition processes; disturbance to and destruction of local ecologies; and the loss of scarce, usually low-income, housing contributing to shortfalls in housing stock. (Imrie, 2021: 30)

Imrie calls this way of thinking the 'demolition paradigm', which, he argues, has become an integral part of building practices:

This paradigm dominates most building cultures and serves to propagate the attitude that knocking down buildings and infrastructure is a panacea for many of the social and economic problems found in cities. It regards demolition as a natural and normal process of building, in which there can be little or no construction without the dismantling and destruction of the pre-existing built environment. (Imrie, 2021: 200)

The practices in the house-building industry are reflected in the final house design. Carmona et al (2003: 1) note that most new dwellings in the UK are poorly designed and of mediocre quality and are usually situated amidst 'unfriendly and unattractive environments dominated by large areas of hard surfaces'. Imrie (2021: 294) notes that 'volume housebuilders tend to construct dwellings for an idealised nuclear family that, if it ever did exist, does not reflect the makeup or the fluidity of contemporary households, or the varied and changing ways that people seek to use domestic spaces'.

Imrie (2021) argues that building practitioners have limited knowledge of, or training about, the interrelationships between a building's form and materiality and people's sensory and cognitive functioning. He cites the smells, sounds and textures of houses and their immediate environments and their impact on the bodily reactions and feelings, including people's emotional and mental wellbeing. The lack of concern with this in dwellings is contrasted to the knowledge that people's mental health is improved by access to nature and natural light and air. Imrie concludes that:

The buildings and spaces that people inhabit are integral to their functioning and wellbeing, yet there is evidence that much of the built environment fails to provide the support and care that is needed to achieve that. There is often a dissonance between constructed environments and basic biological functioning, characterised by the design of places that are not well attuned to natural bodily rhythms such as sleeping and waking, alertness and inattention. (Imrie, 2021: 308)

Imrie's critique and focus on the sensory elements of building materials and the sensitivities and feelings of the humans that interact with them is a vital factor that is usually ignored in many research studies. Wilber's categorisation of the interior elements of a holon is relevant here and the research focus on them is a key part of the analysis of practices advocated here. The result of an application of this approach would be a deeper understanding of the quality of home environments based on the wellbeing and capabilities of the humans that live there, which could have substantial impact on the criteria used to choose appropriate building materials. An extension of this approach to the plants and animals that inhabit the building site and the constructed house would aid understanding of the impact on them of the process. Application of the framework advocated in this book would involve a reconciliation or integration of the scientific analysis of the features of the materials used, for example their strength under load, with information on the cost and ease of use with the sensory and interior elements to provide a holistic picture for the evaluation of the impact of their use in a particular context, both on the house itself and its surroundings and on the wider environment.

The negative views of the processes and the outcomes of house building noted by Horne, Imrie and Carmona may be a function of their context (two are in the UK and one in Australia) and need to be backed up by more extensive research using the practices framework in these and other national contexts. The views may seem surprising given the outlooks and working practices of key professional groups such as planners or architects. Planners have recognised the impact of settlement on climate change and biodiversity for many years perhaps going back as far as the work of Ebenezer Howard on garden cities (Howard, 1898). (For reviews of planning in the UK see Cullingworth and Nadin, 2006, or Parker and Doak, 2012.) The concept of sustainability has been an important element of planning thought, policy and practice, although this has been watered down in recent years as the planning process has been attacked by neoliberal governments as a major obstacle to development. Much of the focus of planners has been on the settlement pattern, which is discussed in the next chapter, but in the UK, planners have some powers of regulation over the house-building process that will vary in different constituent countries. For example, in some circumstances, planners can insist on the provision by developers of a survey of the flora and fauna on a potential site and can lay down planning conditions to preserve existing habitats or to reinstate some features. Some environmental features such as certain trees or habitats can be given protected status. In addition, environmental health officers have the powers to intervene in some circumstances if construction activity is held to constitute a threat to health or to environmental conditions. Building inspectors can regulate the use of building materials and the construction processes involved through the mechanism of building regulations. The contrast between the potential of regulation and the actual outcomes needs to be researched using the practices framework so that the interactions involved in working practices can be disentangled and the key factors leading to negative outcomes identified.

Another major profession involved in the building process that have environmental issues at the core of their professional discourse is that of architects. There are many buildings designed with climate change and biodiversity in mind such as the examples of zero-carbon homes. There are examples of guides to the evaluation of buildings and settlements such as those provided by organisations such as Urbed in the UK and suggestions for how development could be planned and undertaken with regard to its impact on human health and on the rest of Nature (Lawrence, 2021). There are questions about the extent of the acceptance of these ideas within the architectural profession and it is evident that volume house builders in the UK do not often use architects as they prefer to rely on a few standard house designs that they apply in different contexts. Where architects are employed, their influence in the building outcomes in relation to other professions and the financial context within which they are working is unclear and probably varies between situations. The inhabitation practices framework is a good way of charting and understanding how the working practices of architects fit into the relationships that make up overall building practices and the influence this has on the outcome of the constructed house.

The outcome of house development and construction is visible in the house constructed, as well as the myriad other impacts of the process on Nature, including humans, materials and animals. It is important to understand how these impacts occur, particularly if it is thought necessary to change them as we have argued here. Although the development process reaches its climax on the building site, there are a number of processes that influence what happens there. The inhabitation practices approach is well suited to the study of these processes. The working practices of organisations, occupations and professions containing their human, material and animal elements, as well as the relationships between them, are vital elements of the development process. The focus on the building site can be a useful start for the identification and study of these working practices, but they may demand detailed study on their own because of the complexity and large scale of the full picture. We need to identify and understand the individual pieces of the jigsaw before we can see the complete picture.

The discourse of housing shortage

Imrie argues:

> A fallacy of our building culture is that there is a shortage of housing which is the root cause of a crisis that includes unaffordability and

homelessness. A proffered solution is to build more housing, a supply-side argument that … 'is not a simple mistake … it is deliberately and dearly held'. So much so that it goes more or less unchallenged, and it propagates swathes of volume house building that do little to tackle the problems of housing shortfall. (Imrie, 2021: 31)

The discourse of housing shortage is ubiquitous. Clapham (2019) shows that it is a common feature of countries that adopt a neoliberal policy paradigm and that it is closely aligned with the dominance of the market discourse with housing seen primarily as a marketable commodity, and government activity focused on supporting market processes. The causes of the supposed housing shortage are often put down to existing forms of state intervention such as land use planning regulations that are said to stifle the development of new housing. Imrie (2021) sees the housing shortage discourse as one aspect of what he terms 'growthism' in building in general. He sees this as an urge to continually renew buildings and their infrastructure through demolition and new building as more profitable alternatives become apparent.

Like other discourses, the discourse of housing shortage includes a definition of a problem (the lack of affordable housing for some groups in the population); a set of stipulated causes of the problem (the lack of new private house building because of inappropriate public intervention in the market); and a set of policy prescriptions (deregulation and stimulation of housing demand). Therefore, the importance of the discourse of housing shortage is that it sets the agenda for policies and programmes and justifies the actions of governments, house builders and other groups. In other words, it sets the context for inhabitation practices of consumption and production.

Imrie (2021) labels the discourse a fallacy and it is easy to highlight the inaccuracies and inappropriate assumptions involved. For example, Clapham (2019) discusses the many problems caused by the discourse and that it makes the supposed problem it is designed to solve worse by leading to high house price increases and inappropriate new build that does not meet the needs of those with affordability problems. There is no evidence that adoption of the discourse in practice solves the problems it is said to do. This is clearly an issue for political debate and action and the exposition of an alternative discourse or discourses that are aimed more accurately at housing problems.

But the discussion here focuses on the issue most important to our aim in this book, which is the impact of the discourse on the rest of Nature through inhabitation practices. It was argued earlier that practices are composed of human, animal and material elements. Discourses can take many forms. They may exist as materials such as the written word on paper, as recorded speech or on computer memories. It also exists in material form in the brains of human actors. But primarily discourse is one of the factors that is carried by humans in their preparedness to act in particular ways. It is embedded in their 'worldview' or way of perceiving and understanding the world that structures their actions and is a key part of structuration. Therefore, the impact of discourses can be seen in the inhabitation practices of which they are a part.

The study of inhabitation practices needs to include the study of the discourses and this can take two complementary forms. First, there is a need to describe and analyse the discourses as they are expressed at a general level in documents and speeches and government policies, through techniques such as discourse analysis. This helps to delineate and define the discourse and enables it to be linked to outcomes. In the case under consideration here it is possible to compare the expected outcomes in the form of hypotheses about what would be expected with the final outcome in terms of the built form or general consumption outcomes such as energy use and so on. This may then be compared with the expected outcomes of different discourses. A more detailed examination of the inhabitation practices will show the mechanisms that provide the link between the discourse and the outcomes. In other words, it will show how the discourse is refined, changed and acted upon in the context of specific relationships with human, animal and material elements. It follows that any analysis of an inhabitation practice should include the elements of discourse that shape it.

Production practices and policy

The production practices outlined in the chapter result in the outcome of the built form of housing and so are instrumental in housing quality. Many of the regulations that cover the building process such as space standards and the prohibition of hazardous materials are aimed at the health and wellbeing of the future residents. In the previous chapter the importance of homemaking practices to the definition of housing quality was discussed and the concept of capabilities suggested as a way of considering this. This chapter draws attention to the important impact of production practices on this and to highlight the link between the built form and the consumption practices of homemaking that take place in a dwelling whose form will influence them. The practices framework enables an approach to the definition and measurement of housing quality that is based on the desired practices of households and the full spectrum of factors that influence these such as interior as well as exterior elements. Regulatory mechanisms such as building codes can then incorporate these into standards that provide the physical spaces and layout that enable households to undertake valued practices. In some countries a similar approach has been taken to standards designed to overcome disabling environments and layouts that may prevent some people (such as wheelchair users) from undertaking basic activities such as bathing or cooking or moving around the accommodation. The practices framework coupled with use of the concept of capabilities would allow this approach to be expanded and developed to include more people and activities in order to increase the level of housing quality.

Other regulations on the built form are aimed at environmental issues and particularly energy use. The existence of higher levels of insulation and more efficient heating systems removes obstacles to the control of energy use, even though, as we saw in the previous chapter, the eventual outcome will depend on the homemaking practices of residents. But many of the factors identified here are not controlled to the same extent as energy use. For example, issues of biodiversity and the use of materials that are scarce or have high embedded energy or high impact in terms of their extraction or manufacture are not controlled in many countries. The application of the practices approach provides the information that enables the full impact of house construction on the rest of Nature to be described and evaluated and, therefore, could form the basis of decisions about the need for controls. Also, the practices approach can help to identify the relationships and elements that influence the shape of practices and their outcomes and so help in the search for policy mechanisms that will influence these. This should enable interventions to be more effective at targeting the factors that lead to undesired outcomes, rather than relying on inaccurate assumptions about rational actions or economic incentives. For example, a problem may stem from the working practices of one of the professionals involved or the incentives embedded in the working practices of one of the organisations. It is more likely that a problematic outcome may be the result of established relationships between the actors that have been in place for long periods of time and are resistant to change. It was argued earlier that production practices in many countries are perceived by governments to lack incentives to change established practices and to be resistant to their exhortations to change in desired directions.

One of the major factors that provides the context and the 'connective tissue' for production practices is the discourse of housing shortage that was discussed in this chapter. Imrie (2021) links the discourse with the deregulation involved in the dismantling of land use planning controls in England and the increasing pressure to build more new houses. This can also be linked to the pressure for demolition on the grounds of increasing densities and yields on land. The impact on the use of materials and energy use and so on climate change is clear. This links to the observation by Horne (2018) that the reductions in energy consumption made through the introduction of more insulation and more efficient heating systems in houses have been offset by the increased number of houses. The result has been an increase in total energy consumption at the domestic level. Some increase in the number of dwellings may have been necessary to meet population increase, but some has been the result of increased income and wealth inequality and the use of domestic property as a wealth creation mechanism.

This chapter has focused on production for the owner-occupied sector because of its importance in the supply of new housing in many countries. However, the practices approach is applicable to understanding processes and outcomes in different sectors such as public or voluntary housing and there may be reasons that governments may wish to focus support on these sectors because of their accessibility and affordability to certain sectors of the population. In addition, a study of practices may show a difference in outcomes for people, animals and materials between sectors. In his exploration of design for a built environment that meets health and wellbeing outcomes and 'keeps nature in mind', Lawrence (2021) focuses in his chapter on housing on co-operative and collective housing as examples of a decommodified approach that is argued to change the relationship between people and their houses in favour of a more personal connection. This follows the argument of Turner (1976) and others that involvement in the construction process improves the wellbeing of inhabitants. Investigation using the practices approach could test this hypothesis and help to understand why and in what circumstances this is the case as well as including the animal and material elements in the analysis. Therefore, the practices approach can help to guide governments on their tenure policy.

Conclusion

The chapter has discussed the application of the practices approach to the production of houses – a subject that has received far less attention than the homemaking practices discussed in the previous chapter. Nevertheless, the chapter shows that the approach is very relevant to production processes and can lead to useful insights. The importance of the topic to discussions on the role of housing in Nature has been shown in the chapter and takes many forms. The construction of houses uses many materials that are in short supply, and their extraction and manufacture can consume much energy and result in pollution and habitat destruction in the extraction site and in the process of transport to the building site. The process of building can have many impacts through noise and particle pollution as well as impacts on local flora and fauna. Preparation of the site and the possible demolition of existing buildings also has an impact. The effect of the built form on ongoing consumption practices is also important as it will be one of the factors to shape their impact on the rest of Nature.

The practices approach views the production process as a bundle of practices that are performed by actants including humans, materials and animals, and connective tissue such as discourses that bind them together. The human actants include many different professions and organisations, each with their own working practices that are reconciled into one overall practice or bundle of practices that is complex and difficult to untangle. For example, trying to discover the factors that lead to a particular outcome of housing design can be difficult because of the number of elements involved and the complex relationships between them. However, one of the major values of the approach is that it is flexible and holistic enough to enable such a complex array to be described and analysed. Despite this lack of attention to production processes in the practices literature, the chapter has attempted to show the value of the approach and this is illustrated in a number of ways.

First, the practices framework provides a way of charting and understanding the many elements involved in the production process and the relationships between them. This is necessary in order to understand the factors that are important in shaping the outcomes, which should help in the design and implementation of policy mechanisms that seek to change them in terms of the type and number of dwellings built and the impact on the rest of Nature.

Second, application of the framework, together with the concept of capabilities, offers a way of defining the concept of housing quality that is based on the valued homemaking practices of households. Housing quality can then be used as a guide to the forms that the built form can take in order to increase the health and wellbeing of the inhabitants.

Third, the practices approach highlights the impact of the discourse of housing shortage and the impact this has on housing production and on the rest of Nature. As was discussed in this chapter, the discourse was a prominent element in the neoliberal approach housing policy and is a common feature in many countries that have adopted this approach (see Clapham, 2019). The neoliberal discourse and the policies (or lack of them) that flow from it have been blamed for a number of housing problems including affordability and homelessness (Clapham, 2019) but its impact on Nature is also very important as the analysis in the chapter shows. For example, the reduction in domestic energy use that is necessary to meet climate change targets will be difficult to meet by reducing the average energy usage if the total number of dwellings and the total domestic space increase at a level to offset this.

7

Out of home inhabitation practices

In the previous two chapters the focus has been on the inhabitation practices involved in the creation of the dwelling and consumption within it. But inhabitation is also undertaken in a number of locations outside the home. For example, we may leave the home to work and earn an income to pay for consumption within it and to purchase goods that may be used in the home. Children and adults may leave the home for educational activities in schools or universities. Some of our leisure time may be spent in the countryside or in cinemas or restaurants. We may also travel to the homes of friends and family to socialise together. As Horne (2018: 7) argues: 'imposing a boundary around a dwelling and its residents constrains our understanding of sustainability and carbon. We must think of the carbon associated with residents' mobility (getting from place to place) so that the act of dwelling – and scale – must extend to the neighbourhood and the city'. Therefore, a dwelling should be judged on its relationship to other dwellings and to other facilities and the study of inhabitation processes should not be confined to those undertaken at home, but include the activities of daily living located outside and in other locations. Inhabitation practices occur both in the home and in other locations such as neighbourhoods and cities. Maller (2018: 111) draws attention to the importance of cities as a habitat for non-human species of animals and plants and argues that 'all cities, regardless of their size, geography, degree of urbanisation and density (among other characteristics) provide a range of habitats that can support a surprising array of non-human species'. These are most obviously parks and gardens but can include buildings, landfill stations and sometimes areas that contain pollutants that are poisonous to humans, but which can be tolerated by certain plants and animals. As a consequence, cities need to be reframed as a habitat for more than just humans and analysis of practices in the city needs to be aware of the material and animal elements.

It was pointed out in Chapter 1 that inhabitation is undertaken in a number of locales and one reason for the choice of the concept is that it is robust enough to be able to be applied in this situation. It is difficult to make a clear cut-off in what is or is not an inhabitation practice as it could be defined to include the whole of life, so decisions can be made on the basis of importance to issues such as climate change and material use as well as the impact on the capabilities of the people involved. Those involved in the housing field may want to define the limits in terms of the extent of the link to the house or predominant locus of inhabitation. The practical reason for this wide inclusion of locations is clear from the trade-offs involved. For example, reductions in energy use in the home could be offset if a household has to travel further to access employment or other activities. This travel could also have substantial impacts on material use, such as the burning of fossil fuels, the increasing wear and tear on cars, the provision of new public transport that will involve the use of materials and energy and may have an impact on local ecologies. Activities undertaken in the dwelling such as purchasing goods on the internet also have an impact through their delivery to the dwelling. One of the key aspects is the location of the dwelling and its impact on inhabitation practices. There may be important trade-offs for households between housing quality and affordability and location to employment and other facilities. For example, they may have to move further away from the city centre to be able to afford the house they want, but this may result in increased commuting and energy use as well as time spent on other practices.

Niblett and Beuret (2021), in their collection of essays, pose the question of why people travel. The reasons given in the previous paragraphs focus on what they term 'travel as derived demand'. That is, people only value travel outside the home for the functions or activities that the travel affords such as the provision of food and so on. The journey itself is viewed as the neutral means to the desired end and Niblett and Beuret (2021) argue that this is the predominant assumption in the economics and general analysis of travel behaviour. However, as a counterpoint to that view, chapters in their edited collection point to the genetic, cultural and psychological reasons that people value travel for its own sake. *Homo sapiens* has not always lived in settled dwellings with hunter-gatherers moving with the seasons and the availability of food. Settled living only developed with the change to farming. Pasternak (2021) argues that the desire to travel is 'hardwired' into humans and that they have a curiosity that has a physical and psychological basis in the evolution of the species. Active travel has physical and psychological benefits to health and wellbeing of the traveller and allows the curiosity that drives human invention to flourish. Niblett (2021) argues that travel has been seen to broaden the mind, provide self-knowledge and to lead to scientific and artistic discovery. Hiss (2021: 50) states that 'on a deep level the desire to travel is built into us and forms a central part of our wellbeing'. Therefore, people may leave their home for utilitarian reasons (such as to buy food) as well as for the intrinsic joy or inherent desire involved in the travel process itself. As will become apparent in the example of travel to the countryside explored later in the chapter, the reason for travel can have important consequences for public policies that are attempting to reduce energy use by changing travel behaviour.

Much travel is made possible by technology in the form of cars or buses and so on as well as the infrastructure of roads or railways. Also, technology may make a form of travel available to people without leaving their homes or remove or reduce the need for travel. It is now possible for many people to order, receive and consume restaurant meals without moving from their sofas. Television and other technologies may provide some of the benefits of travel through images and description that may reduce the perceived need to travel or alternatively whet the appetite. A recent example of the importance of technology is the availability and use of drones that enable images to be viewed on the ground on a screen. The use of motor-homes has allowed travellers to create a 'movable home' away from the usual dwelling. Such technologies may reduce or increase travel and may change its nature.

The perceived need to reduce carbon footprints has led to a number of policy programmes and discourses aimed at changing the distribution of dwellings in relation to other facilities in order to reduce travel. There has been discussion and action to increase the density of development to reduce travelling. The idea of mixing uses within neighbourhoods is also discussed, with a recent version of this being the '20-minute (or sometimes 15-minute) neighbourhood' where facilities should be available within a 20-minute travelling time on foot or bicycle.

The intention in this chapter is to outline how the inhabitation practices approach can be applied to other locations as well as the home. As in the previous two chapters on production and consumption of dwellings, there are difficult choices to be made about the focus of any study and a diverse approach will be recommended so that the practices and their impact can be examined from a variety of angles and the choice will be determined by the objectives of the specific research study. Three examples will be given in the chapter in order to show some possible approaches. The first is to focus on the redevelopment site in a similar way that was suggested in the previous chapter for the building site. The second example is to focus on a particular inhabitation practice and to follow this through. The example chosen here is the practice of communing with nature. The third example is the examination of discourses as connective tissue that influence many practices. The example here is the related concepts of urban densification such as new urbanism or the '20-minute neighbourhood' that influence public policies and the practices of developers. Finally, the impact of these (and other possible topics) on public policy issues will be considered.

The redevelopment site

As with the building site considered in the previous chapter, a redevelopment site may be a good starting point for the analysis of the inhabitation practices involved. 'Zooming in' on one example in detail (Nicolini, 2012) can lead to a 'zooming out' to follow the factors that have shaped the practice. The redevelopment site may be associated with the same impacts as the building site in terms of the dust, noise and disturbance of the local ecology and redevelopment is likely to be associated with demolition and the impacts this has. New building will lead to an impact that the residents will make on inhabitation practices both within and outside the home. Whereas in the previous chapters the focus was on the home and its immediate environs, in this chapter the emphasis is on the wider impacts of the inhabitation practices outside the home. The location of the development and its density will result in travel behaviour that will consume energy and create impacts on the environment in the locations travelled through as well as the destinations such as city centres, leisure centres or friends' houses. Redevelopment adds some new dimensions to the analysis as there will be an existing resident population that will have to be rehoused in the short and longer term. In the short term, the existing residents will probably have to relocate to another dwelling and possibly area. This may be a permanent move or they may be able to move back into the new development. Horne (2018) points out that many low-income families will be forced to move to the edge of cities to be able to access affordable housing. However, the costs of travelling large distances to access facilities may increase and more than offset the reduction in housing costs, making this outcome financially and environmentally unsustainable. Horne (2018: 158) argues that 'there is an overwhelming brutality in the forced displacement and selection processes of gentrification'.

> In countries with weak tenancy rights such as Australia and the UK, vulnerable residents get unceremoniously evicted from places of lifelong experience and familiarity. During the process, such residents experience a sense of loss, their way of life is undermined, social and physical changes accelerate around them, and prospects become clearer yet darker. This, often drawn-out process, culminates in their spiralling out to the only places they can afford – the distant, ageing, unwanted and peripheral suburbs with few services and few friends. This is the 'symbolic violence' (Atkinson, 2015) of gentrification in home-ownership societies with hollowed-out social and public housing systems. (Horne, 2018: 158)

There may be differences in the number of dwellings in the redevelopment through increased density and so there may be new residents. The material form of the new dwellings may lead to some people performing different inhabitation practices that have different environmental impacts. This change may be influenced by the physical form and equipment within the new dwellings, the changing financial position of the residents because of the price of the new dwellings, or reflect the increased density or facilities in the new layout. Although individual practices will vary, new residents may have different practices because of their previous experience, ethnicity or social class. This may be an important point as many redevelopment schemes have been criticised for changing the social and economic make-up of the locale through gentrification.

There have been a number of important studies of the redevelopment process that have highlighted the economic and social impacts of redevelopment such as Watt's (2021) study of the redevelopment of public housing estates in London. He shows the difficulties of the redevelopment process and its impact on residents who have to live through it. He shows how the, often long, process sets in train a degeneration of the estates in physical and human terms. Before redevelopment, many residents were proud of their association with the area, despite sometimes negative perceptions from those outside, but the redevelopment process seemed to reinforce stigma while losing the community spirit and neighbourhood ties that counteracted this for many residents. Residents who stay on site have the problems of living on a building site with all of its noise, pollution and dislocatory impacts as well as losing the human ties and contacts that existed before. Inhabitation practices may have had to be changed and remade because of changes in the social and physical environment, often on a temporary basis as the redevelopment processes unfolded. Watt (2021) showed the complex pattern of life before and after redevelopment and how this varied between people depending on their situation. But the lack of a holistic conceptual framework through which to describe the findings and to develop the analysis means that many elements are missed and the use of the inhabitation practices approach will enable this analysis to be expanded and deepened to include the total impacts on the human, animal and material elements of the changes brought about by redevelopment. The arguments for and against redevelopment have largely been made on economic and social grounds. The analysis of the economic impacts has mainly been around the land values before and after development and the cost of the additional dwellings produced. The social analyses have focused on the views of the residents on the process (including the existence and scope of participation and consultation) and the general impact on their lives. Adoption of the inhabitation practices approach would deepen the analysis by examining the specific practices that were changed, providing more detail on the nature of changes. Also, the inclusion of material and animal elements would add a different dimension to present analyses. After redevelopment of an estate, a number of elements may have changed including the social make-up and its meaning to residents, as well as the physical layout and the material nature of the dwellings and their surroundings. The inhabitation practices involved may be changed by all of these factors, and it would take a detailed practices analysis to unpick the different influences. Therefore, the practices approach would add to the existing approaches in examining in more detail the social impact of redevelopment that has framed the academic and policy debate.

The inclusion of the material and animal elements means that it is possible to widen the debate on redevelopment to include its impact on the rest of Nature. The material use in redevelopment and its impact on the environment on the redevelopment site as well as the extraction sites and the embodied energy in extracting, fabricating and transporting the building elements will be similar to those discussed in the previous chapter. Changes in the physical fabric of the new dwellings created may influence inhabitation practices and so change energy use through better insulation and heating or cooling systems, although the changes will depend on the interaction between humans and the material elements.

Redevelopment offers a useful focus for analysis as it enables a study of practices before and after the change, providing insight into the different practices associated with intensification and gentrification. However, these two phenomena have been studied in their own right as processes of neighbourhood change. In a later section, the discourses that are used by developers to justify their actions and to market their accommodation, as well as by governments to support these developments, will be discussed and any study of the practices involved in them needs to involve an examination of these. The focus in this section is on the practices involved and their impact.

In the discussion of redevelopment, the change in population and the resulting change in inhabitation practices were highlighted. Gentrification has been shown to involve similar population changes with the influx of new, more affluent households and the forcing out of less affluent households. There may be material changes to the built environment that are associated with these changes such as renovation of dwellings or the opening of new shops or cafes or other facilities as well as policy-driven changes such as in the streetscape or public facilities such as public open spaces. A more affluent population may have different preferences and, coupled with changes in the physical environment and facilities, different social practices may ensue. Most attention in the research on gentrification has been on the increasing social segregation and the exclusion of less affluent households and this is a very valuable focus. The use of the inhabitation practices framework allows an extension of this focus in two major ways.

First, the different practices pursued may change the energy and material use and the impact on animals and plants at the location under study and on related sites such as the place of the extraction of materials or transport to the site and so on. An example of this approach was given in the previous chapter in the discussion of the building site as a research focus. Residents may pursue inhabitation practices that involve travel outside the local neighbourhood and so use energy and create environmental pollution. This additional information will enable the discussion about the impact of gentrification to be widened to include the impact on Nature as a whole, rather than just the social elements.

Second, the social element of the discussion can be seen in a different light. Social segregation has been viewed through the lens of the interactions between people of different backgrounds and social class, but a focus on inhabitation practices can link this through to the ways that people live their lives. The impact of segregation of low-income groups has been viewed through the concept of social exclusion and, as argued in previous chapters, the practices framework offers a way of viewing and defining this concept through the concept of capabilities. The competence to undertake valued practices will depend on the characteristics of the people concerned, their preferences and values, their knowledge and their resources as well as the availability of those practices in that locality. For example, certain inhabitation practices may be curtailed or prevented by the lack of affordable childcare in the locality. Segregation can be viewed in terms of the differences in the inhabitation practices that it is possible to undertake in a locality and the competence by residents to participate. Social exclusion can be defined as the inability to undertake socially valued inhabitation practices. This approach can offer insight into the circumstances of disadvantaged households in different localities and whether this varies according to the segregation in the neighbourhood.

Travelling to Nature

There is considerable research evidence of the beneficial impact on the health and wellbeing of people on being exposed to a 'natural' environment. For example, Maller (2018: 102) argues that '[i]t is now widely accepted that there are numerous health and well-being benefits associated with the presence of various types of living non-humans in urban environments'. Examples quoted include the link between tree cover and the incidence of health benefits such as lower rates of obesity, incidence of type 2 diabetes and high blood pressure (Ulmer et al, 2016). Views of parks are also associated with reduced stress and higher life satisfaction (Honold et al, 2016). Interaction with other species is held to improve physical, psychological and mental health (Soulsbury and White, 2016).

The assumption of a lot of this research is that people leave the home to commune with 'nature' to restore themselves after dealing with the pressures of daily life and so a 'natural environment' is seen as a restorative locale. This formulation raises a number of questions. There is a contradiction in the idea of fleeing home for restoration with the findings of much housing research that the house or home is seen as a secure environment that offers peace, a positive sense of identity, comfort and so on (see Somerville, 1992), although there is a recognition that not all homes provide this for all people. Some homes are physically small or inadequate in ways that make them uncomfortable. Also, homes may have negative meanings such as being linked with financial problems, repair issues or stressful (or physically or mentally abusive) situations and relationships. Homes will vary in their access to natural environments as some will have private gardens or have access to private, public or communal natural spaces, whereas others may not provide easy access. People who live in small homes that do not have private gardens may spend more time outside the house than others. However, there is no evidence that those with problematic housing circumstances leave the home to commune with 'nature' more than those with satisfactory housing situations, although the time and financial resources available may influence this. Residential density is another important element in this. Do people who live in dense neighbourhoods leave their house and travel more to commune with 'nature' than those in lower density neighbourhoods and what implications does this have for energy use? Are the reductions in energy use associated with higher density neighbourhoods offset by increased travelling to 'natural environments' for restoration? Following the discussion earlier in the chapter on the inherent desire for travel, it may be that people are leaving the 'routine' of home and fulfilling an inherent desire for discovery and exploration that may have little link to the home itself.

A further issue is the meaning of a 'natural environment'. Health and wellbeing may be improved by walking in a 'green' urban environment rather than walking along a busy street. In other words, trees, grass and flowers may be perceived as 'natural' and restorative. Why do people travel to places like National Parks that may have a wilder feel? Is this a different reaction or a deeper one? Why do many people travelling to wild areas congregate in the more popular and 'urbanised' locations? What elements are people appreciating in the 'natural environment'? Is it the peace and quiet or the nearness to animal and plant life? The answers to these questions may vary between individuals depending on their resources, stage of the life-cycle and identity as well as cultures and social norms in the society. People who live in wild places are more likely than average to suffer from poverty and disadvantage, whether this shows in poor health outcomes and the high incidence of alcohol or drug abuse. In addition, they may be disadvantaged in terms of access to facilities such as healthcare, sports facilities and so on. So, is the 'natural' environment restorative for them?

The plethora of questions shows that there are gaps in knowledge of 'natural' leisure practices, but the answers are important in understanding the impact of the practices on issues such as energy use and Nature in general. The location of people pursuing natural leisure practices will be impacted by their activity. It was mentioned earlier that tourists in wild places will often congregate in specific places or honeypots. In my home area of the Isle of Skye there is a 'bucket list' of about ten places that see most tourism. It is interesting that many of these are associated with films or television programmes and others have fabricated stories about 'fairies' or other myths. Also, many of the sites are popular for taking 'selfies' and are publicised through social media. There is a growing use of drones in order to view the environment and bans have been enacted in some places to reduce the impact on wildlife. All of these factors point to a tendency among some people to increasingly see the 'natural' environment in digital form, whether through a television, computer or phone, whether at home or in situ. As was discussed in Chapter 1, Von Maltzahn (1994) argues that there has been a tendency in modern thought to see humans as separate from nature and to view it in the guise of an 'objective observer' rather than an active participant. It is possible that the use of drones through which to view nature is an example of this detached view as an observer of a different phenomenon labelled 'nature' that is separate from humans. In contrast, Milligan et al (2021) studied the active engagement by older people in wilderness environments through outdoor adventure activities such as rock climbing. They found that the factors that impacted on wellbeing were many and complex and involved a relationship between the senses of achievement and exhilaration from the activity and interaction with the features of the specific wilderness place such as a feeling of 'being close to nature'. In this case participants were not objective observers but active participants in the landscape. Lea (2008) shows that 'retreating to nature' to pursue activities such as yoga and meditation involve an interrelationship between the activity, the location (which is usually in a 'scenic' place) and the intentions and experiences of the person taking part and involves a process in which 'nature' is an active participant. Lea (2008) argues that such experiences problematise the existent modes of dwelling or inhabitation.

These examples raise the general issue of what is meant by 'nature' or a 'natural' environment and the social practices that have formed this. Important questions include how and why we get pleasure from certain kinds of landscape. Why do we like one kind of landscape and not another? (Von Maltzahn, 1994). Most environments that could be labelled as 'wild' have had an influence from people as they have been habitats for hunting or domesticated animal and crop production as well as a living environment. So, what are the key differences between a 'natural' and an urban environment that stimulate travel outside the home and can these features be replicated in urban environments in private gardens and public open spaces or in the streetscape more generally? The use of an IT lens or screen through which to view 'nature' and the 'Disneyfication' of some sites may point to a narrowing of the differences between urban and 'natural' landscapes. Braidotti (2019) uses the clumsy but useful concept of 'natureculture' to remind us that the two elements of the word are inextricably linked. Our use and understanding of the meaning of natural environments is influenced by cultural issues, as writers such as Macfarlane (2007) have shown, and is relational. Character and meaning are inscribed into the landscape by our experience and our intentionality (Von Maltzahn, 1994).

Also, the answer to the apparent contradiction in the meaning and use of locations such as wild places or homes may be overcome through the realisation that certain meanings and emotions can be replicated in different locations. Identity, security, peace and tranquillity may be found in many places and because they are found in the home does not mean that people will not seek out other sites in which to enjoy them in a different way.

The aim of this section has been to show that inhabitation practices can extend to locations other than the home and that there is a need to understand the practices that underpin them if their impact on Nature is to be evaluated. Even if the practices are undertaken in other sites, it is necessary to understand their relationship to the home and practices situated in the home and why people leave the home to undertake them. In addition, it is important to see visitors to 'natural places' as one element of the practices that constitute the place alongside material and animal elements. Insight can be gained from this perspective especially if material and animal practices are seen as the centre of analysis as a way of understanding the interactions that shape the wellbeing of animals and materials.

Neighbourhood discourses

Analysis of the practices involved in travel to and from the home leads to an examination of the discourses (which are themselves practices) that influence and shape them. Previous chapters have focused on the discourses of 'housing shortage' and the profit-seeking or 'utilitarianism' of the private sector that will influence the extent and type of housing development and thus the shape of cities and towns. Both of these discourses encourage the increased density of development so that more houses can be fitted in to the sites available. Previously in this chapter the impact of demolition and regeneration of some estates has shown that increased density is a way of increasing development profits, pushing up land values and changing neighbourhood characteristics. This 'densification' is also seen as a positive way of reducing the environmental impact of housing development and has been associated with a number of discourses and policy prescriptions such as 'new urbanism' and the '20-minute neighbourhood'. This section aims to examine these discourses and to chart their impact on other inhabitation practices.

Horne (2018) uses the term 'urban intensification' to describe what he sees as an increasing turn away from the suburbs and towards city-centre living in many cities in the developed world. This trend has been brought about by changing housing and transport costs and household preferences and lifestyles, but also through supply trends and variations in land prices and the changing profitability of different forms of development in different types of location as we saw in a previous section on redevelopment. Horne (2018: 159) argues that intensification is a developer-led rather than a consumer-led process: 'Thus, urban intensification is an opportunity for capital accumulation that materialises the urbanisation of capital now usurping suburbia. In global cities with knowledge economies and inward, growing populations, re-urbanisation is a profitable enterprise.'

Densification has also been supported by governments that have promoted the residential conversion of commercial and retail properties as well as the redevelopment of existing residential sites and support for the viability of town and city centres. These measures have often been justified through discourses such as new urbanism which traces its roots back to Jane Jacobs' (1961) plea for vibrant cities and has been influenced strongly by environmental concerns about carbon reduction and climate change. Horne (2018: 155) says the discourse emphasises 'urban vibrancy, social mix, proximity, walkability and a sustainable, car-free lifestyle – a counterpoint to apparently empty or underused urban (or suburban) spaces'. Density is seen as an important element needed to achieve the aims of new urbanism and so the discourse has been used to support densification by developers and governments as well as a justification for government policies in transport and land use distribution. Developers have used the discourse in their marketing material for their high-density urban developments as well as justification for regeneration activity.

In the UK there is a long line of policy towards density and the principles of new urbanism in design and layout from the late 1990s onwards (see Carmona et al, 2003). More recently, with the change in government in 2010, there has been a reduction in planning regulation and building in the suburbs has been pursued in tandem with high-density development and justified by the discourse of housing shortage. On the city scale the discourse has been used to further the development of 'eco-cities'.

Out of home practices and policy

The chapter has shown a number of ways in which a focus on inhabitation practices outside the home can inform policy and practice of governments and housing organisations. The first example was the decision-making around the redevelopment of housing estates that has focused on the economic and social arguments about increasing density and social segregation. The practices framework enables other factors such as the impact on the rest of Nature to be examined through a charting of the changes in consumption practices of the before and after populations. This focus is additional to the analysis in the previous chapter of the redevelopment process itself and its impact on material and energy usage.

A second example of the value of the approach was the out of home practices such as travelling to the countryside or 'nature'. It was shown how such practices are linked to in-home practices and should be considered together. The more holistic analysis can inform issues of house and neighbourhood design through an understanding of why people leave home and the factors that can reduce this. An important element of policy discussion around these issues is the density of residential development and the third example in the chapter examined this.

The discourse of densification used by governments and others has environmental concerns as one of its justifications. The primary argument is that densification reduces mobility and the energy consumed and so reduces carbon emissions. Travel to work journeys may be reduced and people may be more likely to walk or use bicycles. Densification, if associated with appropriate mobility policies that offer residents energy efficient and affordable transport options and make walking and cycling safe and a comfortable experience, would seem to offer reductions in carbon emissions, especially when planning policies and practices ensure that commonly used facilities are within easy travelling distance. However, the discussion in this chapter shows how adoption of a practices approach to the issue may cast more detail on this general picture in a number of ways.

First, the discussion of travelling to 'nature' shows that not all practices are likely to be undertaken within easy travelling distance. Residents of small dwellings are likely to spend more time outside the home and the same may apply to those in high-density areas. Therefore, it is possible that high density may encourage more travels outside the neighbourhood if the features that encourage travel are not available. For example, high-density neighbourhoods may lack the peace and quiet and natural features that people seek as 'respite' and so residents may want to see these features more frequently and have to travel further to experience them. As Samuel concludes, the impact of the COVID-19 pandemic has highlighted this issue:

> Parks, green space and walking routes have been well used during the pandemic. Not only as a place for exercise and meetings with friends, but also as a place of escape from overcrowded and uncomfortable accommodation during the summer months. They have been particularly important to those people who lack garden space or balconies or even windows in their homes. (Samuel, 2020: 4)

Samuel argues that the pandemic offers an opportunity to rethink density and the way people move around their neighbourhoods.

A similar situation may occur in other inhabitation practices. Residents of high-density neighbourhoods may be more likely to visit facilities such as bars and restaurants, cinemas and casinos and so on that all use energy. Other energy consuming practices such as internet use, exercise machines and so on may be undertaken within the home, and could be more energy intensive than alternatives such as a walk in a park. Therefore, a practices framework can add information to the debate that can identify the facilities to be provided in high-density neighbourhoods as well as providing a more accurate picture of energy use and potential savings.

Second, the 'environmental' arguments for high density are usually made in terms of carbon usage and the impact on climate change. These are very important issues that demand immediate action, but they are not the only impacts that inhabitation has. Throughout the book, examples have been given of material usage and impacts on the habitats of plants and animals. It can be argued that densification means that development is focused on existing built-up areas and so reduces the need to develop greenfield sites where the impact on plants and animals may be greater. However, as we have seen in a previous section, redevelopment to achieve greater densities may involve a loss of existing materials and extensive noise and air pollution in the demolition and rebuilding process as well as habitat loss in the material sourcing sites. Redevelopment is more likely in high-density neighbourhoods than it would be in greenfield development. Development of any kind has an impact on the plant and animal habitats. The COVID-19 outbreak has shown that increased density may make a population more susceptible to certain unwelcome habitat changes. High density can increase social interaction and so make transmission of illnesses and harmful viruses and bacteria easier. Samuel comments on the impact of the COVID-19 pandemic on high-density residential development:

> Increasing density has been encouraged by planners and urban designers in recent years as density is needed to sustain local infrastructure and to maximise the use of public transport, however this obviously works against social distancing. A new kind of 'gentle' density needs to be defined that offers resilience during a pandemic, a more street based approach. It seems that there is an urgent need for health and built environment professionals to work together to better understand the relationship between density and infection. (Samuel, 2020: 15)

Samuel argues that because of the pandemic her respondents felt that the pattern of housing demand would change:

> There is likely to be a fall in demand for apartments, in particular high rise, with increasing demand for detached homes and properties with outdoor space. The 'revenge of the suburbs' is a new topic of conversation. House builder research is showing that home buyers are now more interested in the quality of the garden than the kitchen which always used to be the priority. (Samuel, 2020: 14)

Third, the drive for densification has not been based on the wellbeing of the residents. There is little information on the impact of high density on the health and happiness of people. However, in their review, Sharifi et al (2021) argue that densification leads to a reduction of the natural environment, loss of urban green space and reduced biodiversity. They argue that the smaller dwellings that usually result from higher densities are less desired and create more stress for residents. Finally, they argue that, as in the London examples studied by Watt (2021), densification may result in regressive distributional impacts that exacerbate urban inequalities. Although the impacts of high density on residents may be offset by the introduction of urban green space (UGS), this may depend on the size, type and quality of the space such as its sensory aspects of spaciousness and serenity.

This raises important issues about the criteria used to evaluate public policies. In Chapter 4, it was argued that multiple criteria were appropriate in judging policies and the choice of a single criterion such as energy reduction or carbon emissions is likely to hide many other factors important to the wellbeing and capabilities of people and other animals and plant life. The examples given in this chapter show how policies have many and diverse impacts and that one of the strengths of the practices approach is the way that it involves an unpacking of the actors and relationships that lead to these outcomes. The approach outlined in Chapter 4 that disaggregates the study of phenomena into the four quadrants identified by Wilber (2000) provides a way of seeing a practice from different viewpoints and so generating a more holistic picture that elucidates the linkages between elements and the trade-offs involved in any policy decision between different objectives and impacts.

Conclusion

The key message in the chapter is that many inhabitation practices take place outside the home, but are closely linked to those occurring within the dwelling. Therefore, any analysis of homemaking practices needs to explore the links to those happening outside the home and vice versa as the material features of the home and the practices enabled within it will influence the reasons for leaving the home and their incidence and duration. The example given in the chapter was the desire to be in 'nature', but many other practices are linked in this way. This highlights a key advantage of the adoption of the inhabitation concept to define the scope of the field because it stimulates the analysis of the links between phenomena that have in the past largely been considered in isolation. Of course, a consequence is an expansion and complication of any research design.

The chapter showed the importance of the inhabitation practices outside of the dwelling in the impact on the rest of Nature. This has been largely considered in terms of energy consumption through mobility, but there are other issues involved such as material use and plant and animal habitats. If people leave their homes to visit 'nature' this will have an impact on the 'nature' they visit. The chapter focuses on the issue of residential density as an important topic to be re-evaluated in this context. Part of the rationale for the intensification of cities through increased density has been the reduced energy consumption through the decreased need for mobility, especially when allied to planning policies (such as 20-minute neighbourhoods) that aim to ensure that many facilities are within easy reach. However, the chapter has shown that a wider range of factors needs to be taken into consideration within a holistic practices framework to identify the interconnections and varied impacts involved. Increased density could come with downsides that could include more frequent travel outside the dwelling as well as decreased quality of inhabitation through greater susceptibility to disease as shown in the COVID-19 pandemic.

Through the examples of estate regeneration and gentrification, the chapter has also shown the value of the inhabitation practices approach to existing areas of research in housing and related studies. The inhabitation practices of existing and new residents and changes that occur through the different material form and facilities of the dwellings and neighbourhood could have a large impact on factors such as energy consumption and plant and animal habitats. The present focus on economic and social factors does not take these issues into account and so the more holistic framework suggested in this book would help to improve the scope of analysis.

8

Conclusion: Inhabitation research and policy

The starting point for the book was a recognition of the impact of housing on the rest of Nature and the contrast with the relative neglect of the issues involved in many academic and policy debates in housing. Where the topic was recognised there was a focus on a few individual issues, such as the impact of the use of carbon fuels on climate change, without a corresponding focus on other important issues such as the usage of non-renewable materials and biodiversity. Even when Nature was considered, the topics covered tended to be seen as separate subjects that were not integrated into mainstream housing research and policy. For example, the decision by the UK government to increase the level of new house building in England did not seem to consider the impact on the rest of Nature through factors such as increased energy and material use. Therefore, the first aim of the book has been to chart the ways that housing programmes and policies are linked to issues involved in the impact on Nature and this was covered in Chapter 1 and in the examples in Chapters 5, 6 and 7.

One of the reasons for the lack of integration of these issues with mainstream research and policy on housing is that the framework used to consider and analyse them was not appropriate or sufficiently holistic to enable all of the relevant factors to be considered together. The first stage in remedying this has been adoption of the definition of the field as being about inhabitation and so overcoming the disadvantages of the commonly used definitions such as 'housing'. The most useful way of investigating inhabitation is through the framework of practices and the application of this was discussed fully in Chapters 3 and 4 and examples of the worth of the application given in Chapters 5, 6 and 7. In this discussion it was argued that the inhabitation practices framework provides important insights into the role of houses and households in Nature, but also, it provides a useful framework for the investigation of traditional housing research and policy issues such as homelessness and housing quality.

In this concluding chapter, the aim is to briefly summarise the main argument of the book, which is in four parts. First is the case for the importance of seeing the impact of housing on the rest of Nature; second is the redefinition of the field through adoption of the concept of inhabitation; third is the argument for the adoption of the practices approach as a research framework; and fourth is the adoption of a holistic research approach to the study of practices that is wide-ranging and by examining issues from different perspectives (including those of materials and animals). Each of these four arguments is considered in turn. Taken together these constitute a radical overhaul of housing research and policy and so the chapter concludes with a discussion of the implications for both.

The importance of 'housing' to Nature (and vice versa)

The starting point for the book was the realisation that questions concerning Nature were not adequately considered in housing studies despite the importance of their interconnections. As Horne has remarked:

> Housing scholars have been slow to link the core topics of affordable housing and universal housing provision to concerns about climate change ... in housing studies climate change has been a low priority and energy efficiency is questioned as an expense that hinders policy development and programme funding towards universal housing provision. (Horne, 2018: 42)

The argument in Chapter 1 started with a critique of the dualism between people and nature that has been a feature of much thought and which has hindered a holistic appreciation of the links between humans and the rest of Nature in the domestic environment as elsewhere. The dualism is reflected in the common distinction between cities and natural environments. It is argued here that humans are part of Nature and that cities are a product of an interplay of human, animal and material elements as is the rural or so-called 'natural world'. Houses and households (the primary focus of housing studies) are an integral element of Nature and so need to be analysed in that context.

In the book, many examples have been given of the key role that houses and households play in climate change and in other aspects of Nature such as biodiversity, material depletion, air and water pollution and so on. The energy use in dwellings is a substantial proportion of overall energy use (although it varies between countries) and the embedded energy in materials such as plastic and concrete is significant. As well as the extensive use of fossil deposits in the making of plastic and other elements in a dwelling, some materials are in short supply and others have important impacts because their extraction causes pollution or the change or destruction of existing habitats for plants and animals as well as humans. The examination of the building site in Chapter 5 shows how these factors combine and the impact that this has on the local environment as well as the wider global environment. The built form of the dwelling and its relationship to other facilities influence the travel behaviour of households and, as a consequence, the energy used in travelling, as well as the condition of the destination environments and those that they move through. Also, Nature is vital to an understanding of housing, because of the changing inhabitation experiences and patterns that are the result of factors such as climate change and the increased incidence of wild weather, flooding and wildfires. The importance of dwellings and their occupation to Nature means that the study of 'housing' should have these impacts at the forefront of analysis and they should be central to issues of housing policy.

The neglect of a concern with Nature is partly due to a lack of integration in housing studies between the human and material elements involved as was shown in Chapter 2. This seems to be a striking omission, given that the interaction between households and the material form of the dwelling is at the centre of many concerns of housing research such as the meaning of home. A dwelling is a complex assemblage of human, animal and material elements. Therefore, a framework that is devised to be appropriate for the study of housing in Nature is also appropriate for many other core elements of housing studies whether or not they have an important impact on Nature. Some of the examples given in the previous chapters were designed to illustrate this point such as questions of homelessness and housing quality. The integration of what here has been categorised as human, animal and material elements is central to analysis of housing issues and so to housing studies and policy. Therefore, the approach advocated here is not just one for specific topics, but is meant to be applied to the full field of housing or inhabitation.

Inhabitation

In devising an appropriate framework for the study of 'housing' the concept of inhabitation (proposed in Chapter 1) has been adopted in the book as a useful way of defining and demarcating the field. Whereas the term 'housing' places a focus on the dwelling, inhabitation includes the context in which the dwelling is formed and situated. It encapsulates a concern with the process of living in a certain space and the impact this has on the habitat of plants and animals. It highlights the importance of the habitats of non-human species and the overlapping nature of habitation as many plants and animals live in what may be seen as predominantly human habitats. Further, it foregrounds the interaction between the human and other elements as a habitat is made up of animal and material elements as well as human ones and a study of a habitat should focus on the interaction between them. As well as the benefit in terms of Nature debates, the term inhabitation places emphasis on the human and material interactions that are at the heart of living in a built dwelling. Therefore, the term inhabitation widens the scope of housing studies to include previously important but neglected issues and it is proposed as the appropriate definition of the field. What is now termed housing studies should be renamed as inhabitation studies and the same change should be followed through at policymaking levels.

Inhabitation practices

If the concept of inhabitation is used to define the scope of the field, this still leaves the choice of the research paradigm. In Chapter 3, it was argued that the practice tradition is the best source for this. Although the initial focus was on social practices, the approach has been widened to include human, animal and material elements. With its basis in structuration theory, the approach is able to include agency and structure in its scope and so to encapsulate a viable theory of power. Also, it builds on the previous approaches of social constructionism and new materialism, as shown in Chapter 3, and so adopts the strong points of each while avoiding some of their drawbacks. There are many versions of the practice approach and analysts are free to adopt their own preferred option, but one was outlined in this book that is useful and insightful to the study of inhabitation.

Some versions of the practice approach focus on the relations between elements in a practice, seeing agency as vested in these relationships. In this book an approach is taken that focuses both on the make-up of the individual actants as well as their relationships, as it is argued that both aspects influence the shape of the practice and its outcomes. Also, the approach advocated here builds on the identification by Wilber (2000) of quadrants that include individual and collective as well as external and internal dimensions of any phenomenon. That means applying this as a guide to analysis of both the individual elements of the practice and to the practice as a whole.

The preferred approach advocated here also seeks to widen the scope of agency within practices by adopting a more flexible approach to the performance of a practice. The traditional approach sees humans as performing a practice through interaction with animal and material elements, which tends to curtail the agency of the latter. The preferred approach here is to see all the elements, including animals and materials, performing 'in' a practice. This formulation takes away the 'ownership' of practices. Humans do not 'have' or 'own' practices, but participate or perform in them alongside animals and material elements. This formulation allows the focal point of the analysis to be flexible according to the research aims. Therefore, the initial focus can be on particular animals or on material elements such as a monsoon.

Within the tradition there is a concern with the elements that bind practices. The idea of a bundle of practices has been used here to indicate that individual practices are linked through location (such as the home), or shared use of time or elements (such as hot water). The concept of homemaking practices is an example of this approach as it is made up of many individual practices such as cooking, bathing, watching television and so on, that take place in the same general space of the home and have competing and complementary features (such as the use of hot water or the use of time). The elements that link practices have been termed 'connective tissue' and can include particular technologies (such as those needed to heat water) as well as discourses. Discourses can be seen as practices in themselves as well as connective tissues that set the context for individual practices. One example given in Chapter 6 is the discourse of housing shortage, which provides a justification for redevelopment and for substantial new house building.

The approach outlined in the book provides a holistic framework that integrates human, animal and material elements in the analysis and so enables a focus on Nature, that can be seen as a bundle of practices of which inhabitation practices are a part. The framework allows what were termed housing processes to be seen and examined in this context and should provide a valuable tool for those engaged in housing research. The practices approach is useful in many situations in traditional concerns of housing research, even when the impact on Nature is not a primary concern as we have attempted to show in the book.

Researching inhabitation practices

The framework advocated here is not easy to operationalise as has been illustrated in the book. Such a holistic and multi-levelled analysis places stress on the design and implementation of any research strategy, because of the extensive scope required. In Chapter 4 discussion of some of the decisions involved was offered, but decisions will need to be made on the basis of available resources and expertise. A number of general comments are made here that are important in the future of inhabitation (or housing) studies.

The approach advocated here involves a broadening of the scope of the existing field of housing studies to include topics, or aspects of topics, rarely considered hitherto. On a personal level, I have been involved in housing studies seminars, conferences and journal publication for over 40 years and I can remember only very few contributions that focus on the impact of housing issues on the rest of Nature. The examples in Chapters 5, 6 and 7 show some of the topics that could be tackled and also the aspects of traditional topics that have been ignored. The neglect is surprising in a field that has valued its link to policymaking concerns, when policy on climate change and other related issues has been given increasing importance in national and international policy debates.

In Chapter 4, the palette of possible research methods was outlined that may be needed to undertake the holistic analysis suggested here. The breadth of the techniques has implications for the knowledge and skillset of researchers. The combination of the external and internal insights suggested by Wilber (2000) means that any research team is liable to need expertise in both quantitative and qualitative methods and the ability to combine insights from each. The need for integration could also apply to academic disciplines, each of which tend to take different approaches to topics. The spectrum of responses to the challenge posed by the need for a holistic research focus would start with multidisciplinary research where insights from different disciplines could be compared and reconciled. A further step on the spectrum would be for interdisciplinarity, involving an integration of disciplines to provide one united approach. The logic of the framework suggested here is for a unified science and the end of social science as a discrete form of enquiry. However, this is unlikely to happen in the short term and would involve a radical change in the training of scientists and, in the short term, the emphasis in the field of inhabitation studies should be on the integration of insights from other disciplines such as building science. The example of the use of energy for homemaking practices (see Chapter 5) shows the need for integration and what can be achieved by its adoption.

The need for a holistic and wide scope of research can lead to difficult decisions needing to be made about the focus of any research study. Although the specific answers will be dependent on the particular aims of each research study and the resources available, the general technique of 'zooming in and zooming out' has been offered here as a way of approaching the difficulties involved. If the primary focus of the research is on a central practice, describing and analysing this will be the first task. 'Zooming in' will then be focused on the elements of the practice using the quadrants identified by Wilber. 'Zooming out' involves identification and analysis of the 'connective tissue' that binds practices such as discourses and technologies. The extent of each of these stages will differ and it may be necessary to concentrate on a small number of possible options and to piece together parts of the overall jigsaw in stages with a number of research projects.

In summary, the critique offered in this book provides a challenge for existing models of housing research in a number of fundamental ways and represent a radical recasting of the field of housing studies as the holistic study of inhabitation practices.

Public policy

The discussion in the book and the examples in Chapters 5, 6 and 7 provide lessons for policy that is related to inhabitation practices. However, the knowledge base is not extensive and so the discussion here has focused on the potential for the future rather than on the making of specific policy recommendations in the short term. Nevertheless, a number of general comments can be made. There has been some policy and political discussion on topics such as climate change and this is very welcome and clearly urgently needed. Without diverting from this vital issue, there needs to be a focus on issues such as air and water quality, biodiversity and future material availability. The example of the building site as a research focus in Chapter 6 highlights the importance of these issues and the relative lack of attention given to them.

Adoption of the practices approach has some important lessons for the way that policy is made. The case has been made here for an integrated study of inhabitation and the same case can be made for policymaking. The examples in the book show the need for a wider perspective on issues such as neighbourhood planning and specifically policies around residential form and density. Debates on the use of energy in travel tend to be considered within the policy field of transport without an understanding of the relationship between home-based and outside home inhabitation practices. Key questions here are why people leave home and what they are seeking by doing so as well as the impact of the built form on their propensity to do this. Therefore, decisions about transport systems, neighbourhood density, layout and facilities, and the standards for new and existing housing are closely related and should be considered together. The practices framework stimulates this way of thinking by focusing on the links between different elements. The use of the Wilber quadrants encourages a wide appreciation of the different factors involved in any situation. Also, the practices approach allows identification of the key linkages that any policy would attempt to use in order to change an outcome. In other words, it enables the drivers of particular outcomes to be recognised and thus provides insight into the important factors that can lead to change in the desired direction. An example from Chapter 5 is the concept of comfort that drives household choices of energy and heating use.

Good policymaking needs a way of evaluating the impact or success of a policy and a recurring theme of this book has been the inadequacy of predominant ways of doing this. In Chapter 1 the drawbacks of making judgements purely on an economic basis through the monetarisation of costs and benefits was outlined. The concepts of subjective wellbeing and capabilities were introduced as alternatives and their application to animals as well as humans discussed. Acceptance of the capabilities approach highlights the choice of functionings to be used in evaluation and how this choice is made, and provides a stimulus for the use of techniques that attempt to examine the effective functionings that people value and are able to adopt. In this way the capabilities approach can relate questions about the evaluation of inhabitation practices to the valued lifestyles of individuals. The capabilities concept fits well with a practices approach as capabilities can be identified and defined in terms of practices. If the desire is to identify a set of essential capabilities that everyone should be able to achieve, then this can be interpreted in the field of inhabitation as the practices that are considered to constitute an acceptable minimum for everyone rather than in terms of physical attributes of the dwelling place which has been the cornerstone of attempts to define and measure the quality of housing. The concept of inhabitation practices gives a framework for an issue that has had little substantive basis since the health concerns of the 19th century. Poor housing can be defined in terms of the necessary practices that are not possible in that setting. Conversely, good housing can be viewed in terms of the possible practices that it enables.

The practices approach, with its inclusion of the animal and material elements, allows a widening of the factors that can be considered in any appraisal of a policy. In Chapter 7 the example of estate regeneration was given. In an economic or financial cost–benefit appraisal, the factors to be accounted for would be largely financial or easily measured in monetary terms. The key question would be whether the regeneration was good value for money in terms of a return on the capital invested. More critical appraisals of the policy have focused on the social impacts of the process and the outcome for the residents, in terms of their wellbeing. A practices approach opens up new perspectives by examining the practices that are changed by the process, both for existing and new residents and for the neighbourhood. Also, the material and animal elements of the practices can be examined, leading to an evaluation of the impact of the changes brought about by the different inhabitation practices performed by residents on the capabilities of relevant animals and on material elements such as the climate and biodiversity.

How should policies change?

The primary aim of the book has been to address questions about the theoretical and research frameworks for assessing how issues should be investigated and policy made. It was argued that the knowledge base was lacking in many areas and subjects and the policy examples in the later chapters of the book have highlighted the gaping holes in knowledge that need to be filled. Also, the book is intended to be of use in a wide range of national contexts and each country will be at a different point in its policies and programmes that impact on inhabitation practices. Despite these caveats, there is worth in drawing together some general points from the application of the inhabitation practices framework explored here.

Animals and materials

The chapter on consumption practices noted that this is an area that has received some welcome attention in policy, mainly focused on energy use and its impact on carbon depletion and climate change. This is a vital area for continuing policy, but the chapter also showed the many other elements of the practices that constitute homemaking that have an impact on the rest of Nature and are worthy of consideration when seeking to improve the wellbeing and capabilities of animals and materials. The importance of animals was shown in practices such as the level of house heating and in garden care. The existence of a companion animal can even restrict access to shelter in some circumstances. The extraction or cultivation of some materials such as the growth of timber or the mining of gravel can impact on the habitat of some animals. The book has emphasised the importance of the wellbeing and capabilities of animals and offered techniques that can be used to judge these. There is a need to ensure that this element is included in public and private decisions and this may require legislation or regulation. General measures that improve the rights of animals may have an impact on inhabitation as in other fields.

The consideration of materials has usually been restricted to the impact of carbon release, or their function in relation to humans, that is issues about efficiency and toxicity. But the use of materials such as concrete that have important impacts on carbon and use constituent materials such as gravel and cement that have important impacts on the extraction site continue. A concern with the wellbeing of materials would help to uncover the impacts of their use and may lead to more efforts to minimise the use of materials in short supply or which have detrimental impacts. This approach needs to be coupled with measures to protect sensitive areas or landscapes. An interesting approach in some cultures has been the investing of what has usually been seen as human rights in material elements such as rivers or landscape features.

The book has shown the value of a focus on the building or redevelopment site as the place where inhabitation practices 'come together'. A similar policy focus could lead to a more effective and coherent approach to assessment of the impacts of house construction on Nature and a focus for regulatory activity to improve harmful practices.

People and Nature

It has been argued at the outset in Chapter 1 that the perceived dichotomy between people and Nature has had harmful consequences. The view that people and their dwellings and cities are not part of Nature reinforces a tendency to divorce human actions from their consequences and to separate humans from responsibility for their impacts on the rest of Nature. The example of travelling to 'nature' in Chapter 7 shows the importance of viewing Nature as a whole. The chapter asked questions about what is viewed as a natural environment and why people travelled there and what they gained from that. Viewing these natural environments as consisting of the humans that visit them as well as the flora and fauna and landscape fosters a holistic picture of the interactions between these different elements and the practices that are performed there. At the same time this approach raises the question about the form of cities as natural environments. Can cities be designed in a way that people gain the benefits of being in a natural environment through the creation or fostering of important features such as open spaces, trees and tranquillity? Decisions about dwellings or the form and function of cities should be taken in the light of the impact on Nature, seen as a holistic and interdependent element. Inhabitation practices in cities need to be viewed as part of Nature.

Connective tissue

The inhabitation practices approach draws attention to the connective tissue that bind together a number of practices. In particular, the book has shown examples of the discourses that have shaped housing policy (or lack of it) and influenced the form and impact of practices. Examples are the demolition discourse at the heart of regeneration practices and the housing shortage discourse that shapes the perceived need to produce more houses. At the heart of these discourses is a view of houses as a market commodity whose worth is gauged by their market value rather than on their use value or their impact on the wellbeing or capabilities of humans, animals and materials. The view of houses as a market commodity is the foundation for neoliberal housing policies that are the predominant feature of most national housing policies and programmes. There is not the space here to critique in full the neoliberal paradigm (see Clapham, 2019) but it is clear that it is responsible for many of the housing problems of inequality, unaffordability, inaccessibility and homelessness that are characteristic features of many countries. Attempts to deal with these problems within the confines of the neoliberal paradigm that prioritises personal freedom over communal interest have resulted in failure and it is this paradigm that needs to be challenged if progress is to be made on the issues and problems identified in the book. The paradigm needs to be confronted directly with an alternative perspective of inhabitation that sees shelter as a feature of Nature that should be judged on its impact on the wellbeing and capabilities of humans, animals and materials, and that has been the foundation of the analysis in this book.

In addition, the study of inhabitation practices uncovers the constituent discourses that stem from the overall paradigm and challenging these will bring particular gains while undermining the overall perspective. There are a number of subsidiary discourses identified in the book that require immediate challenge. The first of these is the definition of the quality of a house that needs to be detached from criteria related to the market price or to some arbitrarily chosen physical attributes that have little relationship to the way that properties are used. Instead, the criteria need to be aligned with those suggested here for inhabitation policy as a whole, namely the impact on the wellbeing and capabilities of humans, animals and materials. This formulation would bring the impact of a house on Nature, whether through energy consumption, the need to travel, biodiversity or the use of particular materials to the forefront.

A further important discourse is that of housing shortage. In many countries there may be short- or long-term discrepancies in the number of houses in the locations that people want to live in. However, the discourse of a continuing and endemic house shortage is currently promulgated in many countries pursuing a neoliberal policy and has a number of harmful effects. As was shown in Chapter 6, the discourse underlies the perceived importance of producing a large number of dwellings with public policy interventions, such as planning restrictions, building regulations and so on as hindrances to this goal. In other words, it is congruent with the neoliberal emphasis on rolling back the state by reducing interventions in the market, whereas these policy mechanisms may play an important role in meeting the wellbeing and capabilities goals that a focus on the impact on Nature will require. Also, the discourse diverts attention away from distributional aspects of housing. For example, in many countries where this discourse is held by policy makers, the number of houses and housing space per person are at record levels, but the extent of inequality in these countries is also extensive. Building new houses is held to be the answer to homelessness, unaffordability and inaccessibility, rather than addressing these inequalities directly. The policy response of increasing building is difficult to operationalise and ineffective if the new houses built are not accessible and affordable for those in most housing need. In addition to these general housing problems, an increase in house building will result in increased energy and material consumption and could undermine any efforts to reverse climate change or biodiversity loss. Therefore, the discourse needs to be challenged if the problems identified here are to be addressed.

Conclusion

The perils of ignoring the impact of human action on the rest of Nature are becoming increasingly apparent, whether in the form of climate change, biodiversity and landscape loss or the spread of disease and hunger for humans and animals. Nevertheless, action by governments and others to counteract the perceived dangers is piecemeal and not at the scale necessary to overcome the problems identified. This book has examined one element of the interactions between humans and the rest of Nature, which is the field that has traditionally been called 'housing'. It is clear that many aspects of this field have important impacts on Nature as a whole, but only a few of these have been recognised and action taken to alleviate them. There are a number of reasons for this which ultimately boil down to the political and economic interests that are locked into the status quo. However, if these are to be challenged, there needs to be clear grounds established and suitable techniques of analysis identified and utilised to provide the knowledge base.

In the field of housing, it is evident that radical change is needed at different levels. At the most fundamental level there needs to be an acceptance of the need to see Nature as a whole that includes human, animal and material elements and their interactions. Human action, whether in the creation of cities or the building of houses, is part of Nature. As a consequence, the housing field needs to be redefined in order to accommodate the range of factors that need to be included in any relevant analysis. The concept of inhabitation is put forward here as an appropriate definition of the field as it places emphasis on the impact on the rest of Nature. Also, appropriate techniques of analysis need to be adopted in order to identify and assess the important factors and the concept of inhabitation practices has been advocated as a framework for achieving this. As well as these changes, appropriate criteria need to be employed to judge inhabitation circumstances and policies and the concepts of wellbeing and capabilities applied to humans, animals and materials is advocated for this purpose. Taken together, these suggestions call for a fundamental recasting of the housing field and its modes of analysis, but it is argued that this is necessary if the challenges that confront Nature are to be overcome. As Bridle argues:

> Our very survival depends upon our ability to make a new compact with the more-than-human world, one which views the intelligence, the innate being, of all things – animal, vegetable and machine – not as another indication of our own superiority, but as an intimation of our ultimate interdependence, and as an urgent call to humility and care. (Bridle, 2022: 83)

References

Atkinson, R. (2015) Losing one's place: Narratives of neighbourhood change, market injustice and symbolic displacement. *Housing, Theory and Society*, 32(4): 373–388.

Baker, T. and McGuirk, P. (2017) Assemblage thinking as methodology: Commitments and practices for critical policy research. *Territory, Politics, Governance*, 5(4): 425–442.

Ball, P. (2022) *The book of minds: How to understand ourselves and other beings.* London: Picador.

Bauman, Z. (1992) *Intimations of post-modernity.* London: Routledge.

Bennett, J. (2005) The agency of assemblages and the North American blackout. *Public Culture*, 17(3): 445–465.

Bennett, J. (2010) *Vibrant matter: A political ecology of things.* London: Duke University Press.

Bennett, J. (2015) *Systems and things: On vital materialism and object-oriented philosophy – The non-human turn.* Minnesota: University of Minnesota Press.

Berger, P. and Luckmann, T. (1967) *The social construction of reality.* Harmondsworth: Penguin.

Blier, S. (1987) *The anatomy of architecture: Ontology and metaphor in Batammaliba architectural expression.* Chicago: University of Chicago Press.

Blue, S. (2019) Institutional rhythms: Combining practice theory and rhythmanalysis to conceptualise processes of institutionalization. *Time and Society*, 28(3): 922–950.

Blue, S. and Spurling, N. (2017) Qualities of connective tissue in hospital life: How complexes of practices change. In A. Hui, T. Schatzki and E. Shove (eds), *The nexus of practices: Connections, constellations, practitioners.* London: Routledge, pp 24–38.

Boano, C. and Astolfo, G. (2020) Inhabitation as more-than-dwelling: Notes for a renewed grammar. *International Journal of Housing Policy*, 20(4): 555–577.

Bourdieu, P. (1977) *Outline of a theory of practice.* Cambridge: Cambridge University Press.

Bourdieu, P. (1984) *Distinction: A social critique of judgement and taste.* London: Routledge.

Braidotti, R. (2019) *Posthuman knowledge.* Cambridge: Polity.

Bridle, J. (2022) *Ways of being: Beyond human intelligence.* London: Allen Lane.

Burghardt, G. (2007) Critical anthropomorphism, uncritical anthropocentrism and naive nominalism. *Comparative Cognition and Behavior Reviews*, 2: 136–138.

Carmona, M., Carmona, S. and Gallent, N. (2003) *Delivering new homes: Processes, planners and providers.* London: Routledge.

Clapham, D. (2002) Housing pathways: A post modern analytical framework. *Housing, Theory and Society*, 19(2): 57–68.

Clapham, D. (2003) A pathways approach to homelessness research. *Journal of Community and Applied Social Psychology*, 13(2): 1–9.

Clapham, D. (2005) *The meaning of housing: A pathways approach.* Bristol: Policy Press.

Clapham, D. (2012) Social constructionism and beyond in housing research. In D. Clapham, W. Clark and K. Gibb (eds), *The SAGE handbook of housing studies*. London: SAGE, pp 174–187.

Clapham, D. (2015) *Accommodating difference: Evaluating supported housing for vulnerable people*. Bristol: Policy Press.

Clapham, D. (2018) Housing theory, housing research and housing policy. *Housing, Theory and Society*, 35(2): 163–177.

Clapham, D. (2019) *Remaking housing policy: An international study.* Abingdon: Routledge.

Clapham, D. and Foye, C. (2019) *How should we evaluate housing outcomes?* Glasgow: Cache.

Clapham, D., Franklin, B. and Saugeres, L. (2000) Housing management: The social construction of an occupational role. *Housing, Theory and Society*, 17(2): 68–82.

Clapham, D., Foye, C. and Christian, J. (2018) The concept of subjective well-being in housing studies. *Housing, Theory and Society*, 35(3): 261–280.

Cullingworth, B. and Nadin, V. (2006) *Town and country planning in the UK.* Abingdon: Routledge.

Dahl, A. (1996) *The eco principle: Ecology and economics in symbiosis.* London: Zed Books.

Darcy, M. and Manzi, A. (2004) Organisational research: Conflict and power within UK and Australian housing organisations. In K. Jacobs, J. Kemeny and A. Manzi (eds), *Social constructionism in housing research.* Aldershot: Ashgate, pp 142–158.

Dasgupta, P. (2021) *The economics of biodiversity: The Dasgupta review.* Abridged version. London: HM Treasury.

DeLanda, M. (2002) *Intensive science and virtual philosophy*. London: Continuum.

Dennis, N. (1972) *People and planning: The sociology of housing in Sunderland.* London: Faber & Faber.

Donnison, D. (1967) *The government of housing.* Harmondsworth: Penguin.

Dowling, R. and Power, E. (2012) Sizing home, doing family in Sydney, Australia. *Housing Studies*, 27(5): 605–619.

Ellsworth-Krebs, K., Reid, L. and Hunter, C. (2019) Integrated framework of home comfort: Relaxation, companionship and control. *Building Research and Information*, 47(2): 202–218.

Ellsworth-Krebs, K., Reid, L. and Hunter, C. (2021) Home comfort and 'peak household': Implications for home energy demand. *Housing, Theory and Society*, 38(1): 1–20.

Fitzpatrick, S. (2012) Homelessness. In D. Clapham, W. Clark and K. Gibb (eds), *The SAGE handbook of housing research*. London: SAGE, pp 359–378.

Fitzpatrick, S., Mackie, P., Pawson, H., Watts, B. and Wood, J. (2021) *The Covid 19 response to homelessness in Great Britain*. Glasgow: Cache.

Foucault, M. (1972) *The archaeology of knowledge*. London: Tavistock.

Foye, C. (2020) It's about process: Who draws up the list of capabilities and how? *Housing, Theory and Society*, 37(3): 300–304.

Franklin, A. (2006) A post-humanist approach to housing. *Housing, Theory and Society*, 23(3): 137–156.

Gabriel, M. and Jacobs, K. (2008) The post-social turn: Challenges for housing research. *Housing Studies*, 23(4): 527–540.

Gauldie, E. (1974) *Cruel habitations: A history of working-class housing 1780–1918*. London: George, Allen and Unwin.

Gherardi, S. (2017) Sociomateriality in posthuman practice theory. In A. Hui, T. Schatzki and E. Shove (eds), *The nexus of practices: Connections, constellations, practitioners*. London: Routledge, pp 38–51.

Gibson, J. (1979) *The ecological approach to visual perception*. Hillsdale: Erlbaum.

Giddens, A. (1984) *The constitution of society*. Cambridge: Polity Press.

The Guardian (2020a) Bushfires leave 470 animals and 200 plants in dire straits – government analysis. *The Guardian*, 26 April. Accessed at https://www.theguardian.com/environment/2020/apr/26/bushfires-leave-470-plants-and-200-animals-in-dire-straits-government-analysis

The Guardian (2020b) Human impact on wildlife to blame for the spread of viruses. *The Guardian*, 8 April. Accessed at https://www.theguardian.com/environment/2020/apr/08/human-impact-on-wildlife-to-blame-for-spread-of-viruses-says-study-aoe

Gurney, C. (1999) Pride and prejudice: Discourses of normalization in public and private accounts of home ownership. *Housing Studies*, 14(2): 163–183.

Hacking, I. (1999) *The social construction of what?* Cambridge, MA: Harvard University Press.

Heidegger, M. (1971) *Poetry, language, thought*. Translated by A. Hofstadter. New York: Harper & Row.

Hiss, T. (2021) Travel and the mind. In M. Niblett and K. Beuret (eds), *Why travel? Understanding our need to move and how it shapes our lives*. Bristol: Bristol University Press, pp 33–54.

Hitchings, R. (2003) People, plants and performance: On actor network theory and the material pleasures of the private garden. *Social and Cultural Geography*, 4(1): 99–113.

Honold, J., Lakes, T., Beyer, R. and Van der Meer, E. (2016) Restoration in urban spaces. *Environment and Behaviour*, 18(6): 796–825.

Horne, R. (2018) *Housing sustainability in low carbon cities*. Abingdon: Routledge.

Howard, E. (1898) *Tomorrow: A peaceful path to real reform*. London: Swan Sonnenschein.

Hui, A. (2017) Variation and the intersection of practices. In A. Hui, T. Schatzki and E. Shove (eds), *The nexus of practices: Connections, constellations, practitioners*. London: Routledge, pp 52–67.

Hui, A., Schatzki, T. and Shove, E. (eds) (2017) *The nexus of practices: Connections, constellations, practitioners*. London: Routledge.

Imrie, R. (1996) *Disability and the city: International perspectives*. London: Paul Chapman.

Imrie, R. (2004) Housing quality, disability and domesticity. *Housing Studies*, 19(5): 685–690.

Imrie, R. (2021) *Concrete cities: Why we need to build differently*. Bristol: Policy Press.

Ingold, T. (2000) *The perception of the environment: Essays on livelihood, dwelling and skill*. London and New York: Routledge.

Jacobs, J. (1961) *The death and life of great American cities*. New York: Random House.

Jacobs, K. and Manzi, A. (2000) Evaluating the social constructionist paradigm in housing research. *Housing, Theory and Society*, 17(1): 35–42.

Jacobs, K., Kemeny, J. and Manzi, A. (1999) The struggle to define homelessness: A constructivist approach. In D. Clapham and S. Hutson (eds), *Homelessness: Public policies and private troubles*. London: Cassell, pp 11–28.

Jacobs, K., Kemeny, J. and Manzi, A. (eds) (2004) *Social constructionism in housing research*. Aldershot: Ashgate.

Jepson, P. and Blythe, C. (2020) *Rewilding: The radical new science of ecological recovery*. London: Icon Books.

Juniper, T. (2013) *What has nature ever done for us?* London: Profile Books.

Kedward, K., Ryan-Collins, J. and Chenet, H. (2020) Managing nature-related financial risks: A precautionary policy approach for central banks and financial supervisors. Working Paper Series (IIPP WP 2020–09). UCL Institute for Innovation and Public Purpose. Accessed at https://www.ucl. ac.uk/bartlett/public-purpose/wp2020-09

Kemeny, J. (1992) *Housing and social theory*. London: Routledge.

Kemeny, J. and Lowe, S. (1998) Schools of comparative housing research: From convergence to divergence. *Housing Studies*, 13(2): 161–196.

Kimhur, B. (2020) How to apply the capabilities approach to housing: Concepts, theories and challenges. *Housing, Theory and Society*, 37(3): 257–277.

Kirksey, E. (2015) Species: A praxiographic study. *Journal of the Royal Anthropological Institute*, 21(4): 758–780.

Koestler, A. (1967) *The ghost in the machine*. London: Macmillan.

Kohn, E. (2013) *How forests think: Toward an anthropology beyond the human.* Berkeley: University of California Press.

Kotkin, J. (2016) *The human city: Urbanism for the rest of US.* Chicago: Agate Publishing.

Lancione, M. (2020) Radical housing: On the politics of dwelling as difference. *International Journal of Housing Policy*, 20(2): 273–289.

Latour, B. (1993) *We have never been modern.* Cambridge, MA: Harvard University Press.

Latour, B. (2005) *Reassembling the social: An introduction to actor-network-theory.* Oxford: Oxford University Press.

Lawrence, R. (2021) *Creating built environments: Bridging knowledge and practice divides.* London: Routledge.

Lea, J. (2008) Retreating to nature: Rethinking therapeutic landscapes. *Area*, 40: 90–98.

Li, T.M. (2007) Practices of assemblage and community forest management. *Economy and Society*, 36(2): 263–293.

Maalsen, S. (2020) Revising the smart home as assemblage. *Housing Studies*, 35(9): 1534–1549.

Macfarlane, R. (2007) *The wild places.* London: Granta.

Madsen, L. (2019) The comfortable home and energy consumption. *Housing, Theory and Society*, 35(3): 329–352.

Maller, C. (2018) *Healthy urban environments: More than human theories.* London: Routledge.

Maller, C., Horne, R. and Dalton, T. (2012) Green renovations: Intersections of daily routines, housing aspirations and narratives of environmental sustainability. *Housing, Theory and Society*, 29(3): 255–275.

Marston, S.A., Jones, J.P. and Woodward, K. (2005) Human geography without scale. *Transactions of the Institute of British Geographers*, 30(4): 416–432.

McFarlane, C. (2009) Translocal assemblages: Space, power and social movements. *Geoforum*, 40(4): 561–567.

McFarlane, C. (2011) Assemblage and critical urban theory. *City*, 15(2): 204–224.

McGuirk, P. and Dowling, R. (2009) Neoliberal privatisation? Remapping the public and the private in Sydney's masterplanned residential estates. *Political Geography*, 28(3): 174–185.

McKinlay, A., Baldwin, C. and Stevens, N. (2019) Size matters: Dwelling size as a critical factor in urban development. *Urban Policy and Research*, 37(2): 135–150.

Miller, D. (2001) Possessions. In D. Miller (ed), *Home possessions: Material culture behind closed doors.* Oxford: Berg, pp 107–122.

Milligan, C., Chalfont, G., Kaley, A. and Lobban, F. (2021) Wilderness as therapeutic landscape in later life: Towards an understanding of place-based mechanisms of wellbeing through nature-adventure activity. *Social Science and Medicine*, 289: 114411.

Monbiot, G. (2018) The government wants to put a price on nature but that will destroy it. *The Guardian*, 15 May. Accessed at https://www.theg uardian.com/commentisfree/2018/may/15/price-natural-world-destruct ion-natural-capital

Moore, J.W. (2015) *Capitalism and the web of life: Ecology and the accumulation of capital*. London: Verso.

Morley, J. (2017) Technologies within and beyond practices. In A. Hui, T. Schatzki and E. Shove (eds), *The nexus of practices: Connections, constellations, practitioners*. London: Routledge, pp 81–97.

Murdoch, J. (2000) Space against time: Competing rationalities in planning for housing. *Transactions of the Institute of British Geographers*, 25(4): 503–519.

Niblett, M. (2021) Philosophy and travel: The meaning of movement. In M. Niblett and K. Beuret (eds), *Why travel? Understanding our need to move and how it shapes our lives*. Bristol: Bristol University Press pp 55–76.

Niblett, M. and Beuret, K. (eds) (2021) *Why travel? Understanding our need to move and how it shapes our lives*. Bristol: Bristol University Press.

Nicolini, D. (2012) *Practice theory, work and organization*. Oxford: Oxford University Press.

OECD (2003) *Environmentally sustainable buildings: Challenges and policies*. Paris: OECD.

Parker, G. and Doak, J. (2012) *Key concepts in planning*. London: SAGE.

Pasternak, C. (2021) Biological perspectives on travel. In M. Niblett and K. Beuret (eds), *Why travel? Understanding our need to move and how it shapes our lives*. Bristol: Bristol University Press, pp 13–32.

Patra, R. (2006) A comparative study on *Vaastu Shastra* and Heidegger's 'Building, dwelling and thinking'. *Asian Philosophy*, 16(3): 199–218.

Pink, S. (2012) *Situating everyday life*. London: SAGE.

Pitt, H. (2014) Therapeutic experiences of community gardens: Putting flow in its place. *Health and Place*, 27: 84–91.

Plumwood, V. (2009) Environmental justice. In R. Elliot (ed), *Institutional issues involving ethics and justice*. Vol 1. Oxford: Eolss publishers/UNESCO, pp 329–351.

Polanyi, M. (1962) *Personal knowledge: Towards a post-critical philosophy*. London: Routledge and Kegan Paul.

Power, E. (2012) Domestication and the dog: Embodying home. *Area*, 44(3): 371–378.

Power, E. (2017) Renting with pets: A pathway to housing insecurity? *Housing Studies*, 32(3): 336–360.

Quality of Life Foundation (nd) Accessed at https://www.qolf.org/wp-content/uploads/2021/02/PD20-0742-QOLF-Framework_v09_LR.pdf

Reckwitz, A. (2002) Towards a theory of social practices: A development in culturalist theorizing. *European Journal of Social Theory*, 5(2): 243–263.

Røpke, I. (2009) Theories of practice: New inspiration for ecological economic studies on consumption. *Ecological Economics*, 68(10): 2490–2497.

Roth, W. (2018) *Dwelling, building, thinking*. Leiden: Brill Sense.

Samuel, F. (2020) *Impact of housing design and placemaking on social value and wellbeing during the pandemic: Interim report*. Glasgow: Cache.

Sandel, M.J. (2012) *What money can't buy: The moral limits of markets*. London: Penguin.

Savage, M., Bagnall, G. and Longhurst, B. (2005) *Globalization and belonging*. London: SAGE.

Schatzki, T. (2017) Sayings, texts and discursive formations. In A. Hui, T. Schatzki and E. Shove (eds), *The nexus of practices: Connections, constellations, practitioners*. London: Routledge, pp 126–140.

Schatzki, T. (2019) *Social change in a material world*. London and New York: Routledge.

Schatzki, T., Knorr Cetina, K. and Von Savigny, E. (eds) (2001) *The practice turn in contemporary theory*. New York: Routledge.

Schutz, A. (1967) *The phenomenology of the social world*. Chicago: Northwestern Press.

Sharifi, F., Nygaard, A. and Stone, W. (2021) Heterogeneity in the subjective well-being impact of access to urban green space. *Sustainable Cities and Society*, 74. https://doi.org/10.1016/j.scs.2021.103244

Shilling, C. (2003) *The body and social theory*. London: SAGE.

Shove, E. (2003) Changing conventions of comfort, cleanliness and convenience. *Journal of Consumer Policy*, 26 : 395–418.

Shove, E. (2017) Matters of practice. In A. Hui, T. Schatzki and E. Shove (eds), *The nexus of practices: Connections, constellations, practitioners*. London: Routledge, pp 155–168.

Shove, E. and Walker, G. (2014) What is energy for? Social practice and energy demand. *Theory, Culture and Society*, 31(5): 41–58.

Shove, E., Pantzar, M. and Watson, M. (2012) *The dynamics of social practice*. London: SAGE.

Smith, S., Munro, M. and Christie, H. (2006) Performing (housing) markets. *Urban Studies*, 43(1): 81–98.

Smith, T. and Reid, L. (2018) Which 'being' in wellbeing? Ontology, wellness and the geographies of happiness. *Progress in Human Geography*, 42(6): 807–829.

Soaita, A. and McKee, K. (2019) Assembling a 'kind of' home in the UK private renting sector. *Geoforum*, 103: 148–157.

Somerville, P. (1992) Homelessness and the meaning of home: Rooflessness or rootlessness. *International Journal of Urban and Regional Research*, 16(4): 529–539.

Soulsbury, C.D. and White, P.C.L. (2016) Human-wildlife interactions in urban areas: A review of conflicts, benefits and opportunities. *Wildlife Research*, 42(7): 541–553.

Steele, W. and Vizel, I. (2014) Housing and the material imagination: Earth, fire air and water. *Housing Studies*, 31(1): 76–90.

Storper, M. and Scott, A. (2016) Current debates in urban theory: A critical assessment. *Urban Studies*, 53(6): 1114–1136.

Strengers, Y. (2013) *Smart energy technologies in everyday life: Smart utopia?* London: Palgrave Macmillan.

Strengers, Y., Nicholls, L. and Maller, C. (2016) Curious energy consumers: Humans and nonhumans in assemblages of household practice. *Journal of Consumer Culture*, 16(3): 761–780.

Taylor, P.J., O'Brien, G. and O'Keefe, P. (2020) *Cities demanding the earth: A new understanding of the climate emergency*. Bristol: Bristol University Press.

Tonkiss, F. (2011) Template urbanism: Four points about assemblage. *City*, 15(5): 584–588.

Travers, M. (2004) The philosophical assumptions of constructionism. In K. Jacobs, J. Kemeny and A. Manzi (eds), *Social constructionism in housing research*. Aldershot: Ashgate, pp 14–31.

Turner, J. (1976) *Housing by people: Towards autonomy in building environments*. London: Boyars.

Ulmer, J.M., Wolf, K.L., Backman, D.R., Tretheway, R.L., Blain, C.J.A., O'Neil-Dunne, J.P.M. and Frank, L.D. (2016) Multiple health benefits of urban tree canopy: The mounting evidence for a green prescription. *Health and Place*, 42: 54–62.

Von Maltzahn, K. (1994) *Nature as landscape: Dwelling and understanding*. Montreal: McGill-Queen's University Press.

Wallenborn, G. and Wilhite, H. (2014) Rethinking embodied knowledge and household consumption. *Energy Research & Social Science*, 1: 56–64.

Watson, M. (2017) Placing power in practice theory. In A. Hui, T. Schatzki and E. Shove (eds), *The nexus of practices: Connections, constellations, practitioners*. London: Routledge, pp 169–182.

Watt, P. (2021) *Estate regeneration and its discontents: Public housing, place and inequality in London*. Bristol: Policy Press.

Wilber, K. (2000) *Sex, ecology, spirituality: The spirit of evolution*. Boulder: Shambhala Publications.

Index

Page numbers in *italic* type refer to figures.